A Table in the Mist

Meditations on Ecclesiastes

Jeffrey J. Meyers

Athanasius Press

Monroe, Louisiana

A Table in the Mist: Meditations on Ecclesiastes

205 Roselawn
Monroe, Louisiana 71201
www.athanasiuspress.org

To Jeffrey

May God keep you occupied
with the joy of your heart!

CONTENTS

	Preface	vii
1	The Shepherd King's Wisdom	13
2	A Short Primer on Wisdom and Wisdom Literature	25

PART ONE | ECCLESIASTES 1:1–2:26

3	Everything is Vapor *Ecclesiastes 1:2–11*	39
4	Learning from Solomon's Quest *Ecclesiastes 1:12–2:26*	49

PART TWO | ECCLESIASTES 3:1–5:20

5	The Burden of Eternity in Our Hearts *Ecclesiastes 3:1–15*	71
6	Death and Friendship *Ecclesiastes 3:16–4:16*	87
7	Household Etiquette *Ecclesiastes 5:1–20*	105

PART THREE | ECCLESIASTES 6:1–8:17

8	Discerning Good, Better, and Best *Ecclesiastes 6:1–7:12*	129
9	A Riddle Wrapped in a Mystery Inside an Enigma *Ecclesiastes 7:13–8:17*	145

PART FOUR | ECCLESIASTES 9–12

10	Wine, Oil, and a Few Flies *Ecclesiastes 9:1–10:20*	173
11	Bread Upon the Waters *Ecclesiastes 11:1–6*	191
12	The Conclusion of the Matter *Ecclesiastes 11:7–12:14*	203
	Suggested Readings and Resources	219

Preface

As I sit in my quiet basement study writing this preface, the world outside is buzzing with commotion. It is Christmas time. With less than a week of shopping left before the big day, there is a great whirl of activity everywhere. Everyone is frantically making preparations. Businesses are throwing parties. Families are gathering for annual feasts. Dazzling decorations have been strewn over buildings, homes, and even doghouses. Bright lights, evergreen boughs, multi-colored bulbous ornaments, and glittering silver strands of garland garnish windows and doorways all up and down the street. It would seem, from all outward appearances, that everything is right in the world, that peace and joy reign supreme.

But, as everyone knows, colorful Christmas decorations often mask dark depression for many people. Even though the feast of Christmas ought to be a time when even those who have much to be troubled about experience a ray of divine joy and happiness around the table with relatives and friends, oftentimes the season itself exacerbates people's problems. How can this be?

The Christmas holiday season has been increasingly cut loose from its foundation in the Bible and Christian tradition. Modern Christmas seasons provide us with little more than sentimental, syrupy niceness and nice thoughts about a mistily-glowing baby Jesus. All we are left with is the commoditization of vague religious sentimentalism. There is no spiritual power in this. What's worse, because of this the Christian faith seems, to many in our culture, little more than an attempt to stir up comforting religious feelings to mask one's real troubles in the world. But this is so far removed from the Bible and genuine Christian tradition that it has to be considered another religion, one that plays make-believe with the dirty realities of this life.

What does all this have to do with Ecclesiastes? Simply this: when the true faith is robustly biblical, it will also honestly narrate and confront the intractable evil and misery of this life. Solomon records his observations with shocking candor: "Everything is vapor."

Trying to control your life is like "shepherding the wind." "What is twisted cannot be made straight." "No man has power over the day of death." Solomon's frank meditations are not at odds with the gospel story. The biblical Christmas story has the eternal Son of God take on our dilapidated flesh and enter our fallen world as Savior. There is no sugarcoating the bitter social, political, and economic troubles of the world that Jesus enters. Just read the birth narratives in the gospels. Matthew and Luke were wise like Solomon, which means they were honest about the world. Indeed, the coming of Jesus teased out the worst in humanity. After all, in the end the world conspires to murder the innocent Son of God.

What may be surprising to some who are not familiar with the story of the Bible as a whole is that Solomon's lively faith *also* commends dancing and feasting with exuberance, rejoicing in the good gifts that God has provided for his people. "Go eat your bread with joy and drink your wine with a merry heart, for God has already approved what you do . . . Enjoy life with the wife whom you love, all the days of your vaporous life." For Solomon, one can do nothing better than drink wine, enjoy the woman God has given him, and sing and dance with the revelers at the feasts of Yahweh.

Back to Christmas. The problem, then, of course, is not with Christmas, not even with Christmas decorations. It's not that people are too happy or feast with abandon. We should celebrate Christmas with wild, joyous abandon, as Solomon himself would surely endorse. But we must be careful not to allow our feasting to blind us to the reality of the curse. We sing "Joy to the world" because we believe that Jesus has come "to make his blessings flow far as the curse is found."

The Christmas season is wonderful, pure joy. I even love what some derisively lament as "the commercialization" of Christmas. I say, let the brilliant lights multiply and beautify every home on the block. None of this is meant to deny that the world is dark and cold. Christians must be realists about the world and life; the Bible is. The church celebrates Christmas season in the dead of winter for good reasons. Faith does not mean ignoring the "living death," as Augustine put it, of our cursed world; rather, it means trusting

God while confessing our own bafflement and impotence to change our death-stamped existence in this world. This is where Solomon's Ecclesiastes can help us modern Christians. As we shall see, biblical wisdom does not give us the power to leverage the world to insure our own health or success. Death in its various forms is everyone's future. Nevertheless, we can genuinely enjoy life. Joy *and* curse, not one or the other. According to Solomon, the wise man will affirm them both.

And what better way for a Christian to rediscover the spiritual power in honest evaluations of our twisted world and life than to read and mediate on Solomon's Ecclesiastes? In Bradbury's classic *Fahrenheit 451*, the reclusive Professor Faber explains to the curious Guy Montag the "magic" of books. He is holding a very rare copy of the Bible brought to him by Montag.

> Do you know why books such as this are important? Because they have quality. And what does the word quality mean? To me it means texture. This book has *pores*. It has features. This book can go under the microscope. You'd find life under the glass, streaming past in infinite profusion. The more pores, the more truthfully recorded details of life per square inch you can get on a sheet of paper, the more "literary" you are. That's *my* definition, anyway. *Telling detail. Fresh* detail. The good writers touch life often. The mediocre ones run a quick hand over her. The bad ones rape her and leave her for the flies. So now do you see why books are hated and feared? They show the pores in the face of life. The comfortable people want only wax moon faces, poreless, hairless, expressionless. We are living in a time when flowers are trying to live on flowers, instead of growing on good rain and black loam. (Ray Bradbury, *Fahrenheit 451* [New York: Ballantine, 1953], 83)

I can't help but think of the book of Ecclesiastes when I read Faber's description of a good book. Of course, he is holding the Bible as he makes this little speech, and Ecclesiastes is quoted in the story more than once. Solomon's book is the perfect example of literature that shows the "pores in the face of life." The son of David is so honest about the difficulties in life that it scares many Christians, and he trusts God so much he has a bit too much fun—

he drinks wine and actually enjoys sex with his wife! This is way too much "fresh detail" for some Christians.

I am convinced that this is one of the reasons why so many commentaries and sermon series are, in effect, massive efforts to domesticate Solomon's wisdom. His observations, maxims, and advice, we are sometimes told by pious commentators, are the desperate ramblings of a hopeless pagan soul, not the wisdom of a faithful believer. How could a believer be so pessimistic? How could a believer condone such pleasure? So the mantle of a pagan sage is forced on Solomon and the book then becomes simply an apologetic tool to show us that life apart from God is meaningless. But this is a lot like modern escapist Christmas celebrations. It ignores reality. It is a childish and immature way of handling the harsh realities of life, but I'm getting ahead of myself. I invite you to join me in hearing Solomon as he fulfills his vocation as shepherd king of Israel by faithfully communicating the wisdom of the divine Shepherd through delightful words of truth (Eccl. 11:9–14). The mature king invites us to a feast at a table in the mist. At that table we are called to enjoy wine, woman, and song—all gracious gifts of God to be enjoyed by faith.

Acknowledgements

In order to keep the book free of the marks of academia, I have not referenced every source I consulted. I have benefited from many different commentators, only a few of which are mentioned in the text. My hope is that the book will be easily accessible to most Christians, not just academically sophisticated readers.

A heart-felt thank you to all who have helped me write this book. Mark Horne transcribed my sermons and added his own sound advice and comments at many points in the course of his work. Mark's intellectual gifts and exegetical discernment have yet to be "discovered," but for me he has been a trusted confidant and discerning assistant for many years. I appreciate the care he took in helping me with this commentary.

Special thanks are reserved for James B. Jordan. Having now spent many years in theological education, both at Covenant Theological Seminary (MDiv) and Concordia Theological Seminary (STM and PhD studies), I can honestly say that I have never known another teacher who knows the Bible so thoroughly as Jim Jordan. He's been my teacher and a good friend for many years. I only hope this popular commentary lives up to his high standards.

I must also thank the elders of Providence Reformed Presbyterian Church. They have been very generous, gracious, and accommodating to me as I worked on this book. Indeed, this is their standard mode of operation! And without the encouragement of the members of Providence I don't know that it would have ever occurred to me to make the effort necessary to get these comments on Ecclesiastes published. The Lord has been uncommonly merciful to me in giving me such a responsive congregation. Sharing a common Table with such a company of saints has indeed been the best antidote to the misty, uncontrollable existence of life under the sun. I pray that this book will bear similar fruit as more and more Christians embrace the astonishing wisdom of Ecclesiastes.

And finally, I must thank my own wife with whom I have been gifted by God to enjoy life. For twenty-seven years she has been the stability of our home and the source of constant joy for me in this altogether vaporous life. Heeding Solomon's sage advice, we have had many relaxing evenings together over a bottle of wine. The original working title of this book was *Wine, Woman, and Song*. Well, for me two out of three ain't bad—wine and an amazing woman. Now if I could only dance and sing!

Jeffrey J. Meyers
Fourth Sunday in Advent
December 18, 2005

1

THE SHEPHERD KING'S WISDOM

The words of the wise are like goads. —Ecclesiastes 12:11

The wisdom of Ecclesiastes has endlessly fascinated people whether they have understood it or not. While the book's meaning may be mysterious, that mystery has captivated most people who read it, Christian and non-Christian alike. They are enthralled by the book's literary beauty as well as astonished at the elusive nature of its content. Sadly, that fascination has not really helped everyone get a grip on this portion of God's Word.

This victory for Ecclesiastes has actually resulted in a sort of defeat. As has happened all too often with the Bible as a whole, all sorts of clipped quotations from the book have taken on a life of their own to become sayings and stock phrases that one meets in all kinds of contexts that tell you nothing about what the text actually says. The text's popularity has resulted in its dismemberment. Consider how many of these sayings you have heard outside of reading the Bible.

> Vanity of vanities, all is vanity.
> There is nothing new under the sun.
> For with much wisdom comes much grief, the more knowledge the more sorrow.
> There is a time for everything, a season for every activity under heaven.
> Man's fate is like that of the animals; the same fate awaits them both.
> A cord of three strands is not quickly broken.
> Cast your bread upon the waters, for after many days you will find it again.
> Remember your Creator in the days of your youth.
> Of the making of many books there is no end, and much study wearies the body.

It is impossible to be well-acquainted with Western literary culture without having encountered these expressions. Indeed, in some cases they are encountered in popular music from the sixties and in contemporary wedding announcements. In one sense, such quoting is only right and just. The book of Ecclesiastes informs us that the author has sought out, found, and arranged for us "words of delight," and that "uprightly he wrote words of truth" (Eccl. 12:10). He was successful. Yet in spite of our acquaintance with the clever aphorisms of Ecclesiastes, or perhaps even because of it in this popular but scattered form, the book as a whole remains for many an incomprehensible mystery—a huge conundrum smack in the middle of Holy Scripture. What exactly is it that is upright and true about the delightful words of Ecclesiastes?

WHAT IS ECCLESIASTES ABOUT?

Have you ever sat strapped into your seat on a taxiing airplane, wondering how the airport keeps track of all those planes? I have always been fascinated by the amount of air traffic that airports are able to manage, especially large hubs like O'Hare, Dallas-Fort Worth, or Atlanta. On the ground you can formulate a very sketchy idea of the overall plan, but you cannot see all the planes that are being maneuvered and guided according to some hidden plan. You need to be taken up into the control tower. Many years ago I was in an air traffic control tower in Augusta, Georgia. I was the officer in charge of loading a battalion of army signal equipment into C-130s and C-141s that day, and one of the air force officers took me up.

The equipment was not nearly as sophisticated as it is today, but the air traffic controllers were able to look at the entire situation on their screen and interpret lights, numbers, and codes with such precision that they could control the movement of dozens of aircraft from that control tower. Once you see these screens and learn the codes, the rationality of the plan and the reasons why each plane is precisely where it is become plain.

For many people, both Christians and not, that is what wisdom is supposed to be like. J. I. Packer, however, makes the enormously helpful observation that the mistake often made by Christians is to suppose that a train station signal box is a fitting illustration of how a wise man understands the world. The mistake is to think that

> the gift of wisdom consists in a deepened insight into the providential meaning and purpose of events going on around us, an ability to see why God has done what he has done in a particular case, and what he is going to do next. People feel that if they were really walking close to God, so that he could impart wisdom to them freely, then they would, so to speak, find themselves in the signal box; they would discern the real purpose of everything that happened to them, and it would be clear to them how God was making all things work together for good. Such people spend much time poring over the book of providence, wondering why God should have allowed this or that to take place, whether they should take it as a sign to stop one thing and start doing another, or why they should deduce from it. If they end up baffled, they put it down to their own lack of spirituality. (*Knowing God* [repr., 1993, Downer's Grove, IL: IVP, 1973], 92)

The gift of biblical wisdom, in other words, is *not* all about getting a privileged seat in God's traffic control tower of the world. We don't get to understand why things happen the way they do. We are mistaken if we think wisdom gives us that sort of insight.

The other mistake we make about wisdom is to think that godly wisdom gives us leverage such that we can learn to control our lives through the acquisition of biblical knowledge and skill. The idea here is that biblical wisdom is "how-to" wisdom: how to have a successful marriage, how to raise children, how to do business. The outcome can almost be guaranteed if the proper techniques are used. The mistake is to think that biblical wisdom gives one *control*. As Packer writes, "So far from the gift of wisdom consisting in the power to do this, the gift actually presupposes our conscious inability to do it!"

That is the message of Ecclesiastes. What the author intends to teach us is that real biblical wisdom is founded on the honest acknowledgement that this world's course is enigmatic, that most, if not all, of what happens is quite inexplicable, incomprehensible to us, *and* quite out of our control. We cannot leverage the course of the world this way and that to suit our petty purposes. The godly wise man and woman will humbly concede that God has hidden from us almost everything that we should like to know about his providential purposes. Therefore, all of our attempts to influence or comprehend the world and the course of our lives are futile, useless, vain, and empty. Vanity of vanities. The wise man learns to walk by faith and not by sight.

Ecclesiastes is *the* book about faith in the Old Testament. It tells how the man of faith looks at the world. We are told that a wise and faithful person will come to embrace the perspective of Solomon that all of life is "vapor"! The life of faith is not grounded in our ability to discern the meaning of everything in our world. Faith is the assurance of things hoped for, the conviction concerning things not yet seen (Heb. 11).

Life in itself is unable to supply the key to the questions of identity, meaning, purpose, value, and destiny. Only God holds the key, and he must be trusted with it. He does not make copies of the key for us to use. You do not get to keep God's key in your back pocket. Sooner or later, if you are a believer, you are going to have to actually trust God to keep the key to life.

To the extent that we have learned true wisdom, our part as Christians is to fear God and keep his commandments, to receive and use the gifts of God with joy and gratitude, that is, to eat, drink, work, love our husbands and wives, rejoicing in all of these things, all the while knowing that we *cannot* understand his ways and *must not* attempt to play god in his world. We must not try to gain leverage to manipulate the world to our petty purposes. That is the wisdom of Solomon.

LISTENING TO THE SHEPHERD KING

A friend of mine once owned a pretty postcard with a sunset pictured on it along with a pious-sounding Bible verse as a caption. The text was from Job 22:21—"Agree with God, and be at peace; thereby good will come to you." It sounds like a wonderful promise of God—the sort of verse one might find in those little verse-a-day calendars to help you feel good.

My friend, however, didn't keep the postcard for sentimental value. He kept it because it was hysterically funny. It was a classic example of entirely misreading the Bible and of trading true biblical wisdom for a false but shiny wisdom that we find all too attractive and plausible. Like Ecclesiastes, Job is from the kingly period in Israel's history, when King David composed many psalms and then Solomon used divinely-given wisdom to craft many proverbs. And like all wisdom literature, Job has to be read *carefully*. In the book of Job, God strikes down Job in horrible ways. The book then consists of three "friends" of Job trying to get him to admit that he deserves this calamity because he has done wrong. After all, why else would God make him suffer so dramatically? But the book makes it unambiguously clear that Job is in the right and his accusers are wrong. He has done nothing wrong; God is not punishing him.

The punch line is this: it is neither Job nor God who teaches "agree with God, and be at peace; thereby good will come to you" (Job 22:21). No, this claim comes from one of Job's false accusers who is trying to convince Job that he is guilty and is moralistically beating him up in the midst of his tragedy. The makers of the postcard did not bother to track who was speaking within the story of Job or the point of his statement within that story. There are many who would dispute the idea that Ecclesiastes is a book teaching us true Christian wisdom. As in Job, it all depends on who is speaking or what role he may be playing within the book of Ecclesiastes.

The first thing we learn in reading Ecclesiastes is that these words are spoken or written in fulfillment of Solomon's office as chief shepherd and teacher of the people of God. But this important point is resisted in many circles, both because of and resulting in a fundamental misreading of Ecclesiastes. " 'Vanity of vanities.' What can *this* mean?" readers ask themselves. "In what spirit and for what purpose does Solomon propound this aphorism?" Many wish to grasp at some alternative to the view that Solomon is speaking as a wise man. They don't want to believe that Solomon is teaching true wisdom within the human limitations that are common to all people, including believers. So they try to come up with other options.

Is the author an embittered cynic? Is this the last gasp of a selfish and callous old man of the world who finds nothing but disillusionment and despair at the end of his life?

Is Solomon speaking as an unbeliever in order to convince pagans of the utter futility of their own worldview? Is this an attempt to convince people that without God, all is empty, vain, useless, and meaningless?

Is this Solomon speaking as the lapsed one? The one who has temporarily abandoned his faith perspective?

These are very popular views. I suspect that too often something like this is our gut-reaction interpretation of Ecclesiastes. Solomon has either fallen off the deep end—or is pretending like he has—in order to warn others about the presence of the pit.

One of these options was certainly my own view at one time. In 1979 I made some marginal comments in a new Bible my fiancée gave me just a few months before we were married: "This book describes the emptiness and futility of life outside of Christ. For the one who does not know God, everything is vanity." If you don't have faith in God, then life will be meaningless, futile, and vain. I was sure that the author's goal was to show the emptiness of life apart from God. Only with God can we understand the world and life properly. Without the Lord it is all vanity.

I naively thought that when we are reconciled with God by faith we will have no problem understanding the world and life properly. That was what I thought Ecclesiastes was teaching me. This kind of idealistic dream may be the stuff of a 22-year-old Christian's idealistic pseudo-wisdom, but it is most certainly *not* the wisdom of Solomon! His is the wisdom that results from the mature experience of a man of faith. Truth be told, I had not yet read the book very carefully.

While many would deny that Solomon wrote this text as God's chosen king, there is no getting around the clear statement introducing the book of Ecclesiastes: "*The words of the Preacher, the son of David, king in Jerusalem.*" That introduction would not be there at the opening of the book if it were unimportant to understanding what the Holy Spirit is saying to us. Introductions serve a purpose. God could have inspired the book to begin with verse two and excluded any reference to a son of David living in God's chosen city, the capital of the people of God, but he chose otherwise. The introduction in verse one clearly tells us that we must hear or read the book of Ecclesiastes as true royal wisdom. It is true, of course, that Solomon lapsed, but there is no way to escape the implication that the book of Ecclesiastes is being *commended* to the reader as the work of God's king.

The author's self-evaluation in 1:16, claiming to have surpassed in wisdom "all who were over Jerusalem before me," is no argument against Solomonic authorship. Some have thought that this statement is too bombastic for Solomon's situation, since he was only the second king to reign in Jerusalem, but this is not accurate. True enough, he was the second *Israelite* king to rule from Jerusalem, but he was one in a long, famous list of kings to rule from Salem. Among these are Melchizedek, the priest-king who gave Abraham bread and wine (Gen. 14:18), Adonizedek (Josh. 10:1), Araunah (1 Sam. 24:23), and, of course, David. And we are told explicitly in 1 Kings 3:12 that no one after Solomon would be as wise as he.

The words of Ecclesiastes are not the words of a cynic or an epicurean or a humanist or an unbeliever. One can easily infer from the author's status as king in Jerusalem that these are the words of a *pastor*, one appointed by God to shepherd the Lord's flock in wisdom and truth. But there is no need to rely on inference.

In addition to being described as the son of David and the king in Jerusalem, the author of Ecclesiastes is referred to by another title. Sometimes it is translated as "the Preacher," as in the ESV (English Standard Version) of the Bible. In other English translations other words are used such as "teacher." Sometimes people simply transliterate the word as *kohelleth* or *qoheleth*. The Hebrew word is translated by the Greek "ecclesiastes" which means a member of the *ecclesia* or, as we might say, "an ecclesiastic."

The Greek translation is largely on target. *Qoheleth* is from the Hebrew word *qahal*, which means "assembly." The Hebrew word *qoheleth* suggests one who calls together an assembly (*qahal*)—a convener, a gatherer. *Qoheleth* is the one who *convenes* or *assembles* the people together, in this case to teach and instruct in wisdom. Throughout the history of the kings of Israel recorded in Kings and Chronicles we learn that one of the functions of the king was to assemble the people for the annual feasts and for other important national events. When the temple was dedicated at the beginning of Solomon's reign, he gathered (*qahal*) the people for the ceremony (1 Kings 8:1–2, 14, 22, 55, 65). From this information, then, it appears as if the best way to translate *qoheleth* is by a word that denotes the king's office as "gatherer" or "convener." Since this is also what shepherds do with their sheep, it may be best, at times, simply to use the designation "shepherd" to refer to King Solomon's office.

This title again indicates that the author of Ecclesiastes is not some cynic, whether an unbeliever or a backslidden Israelite. This is Solomon speaking in his office as shepherd king of Israel. He is, according to his office as Davidic king, the chief human shepherd in Israel. He is the anointed ruler of Israel fulfilling his office as shepherd over the Old Testament people of God. Remember, the Lord called to David and his descendents: "You shall be shepherd of my people Israel, and you shall be prince over Israel" (2 Sam. 5:2). And in that capacity Solomon assembled (*qahal*) Israel before the temple (2 Chron. 5:1–3; 6:1).

Consider Ecclesiastes 12:10–11 where the book is nearing its conclusion: "The Preacher sought to find words of delight, and uprightly he wrote words of truth. The words of the wise are like goads, and like nails firmly fixed are the collected sayings; they are given by one Shepherd." These are not the words of a cynic, but of a pastor, one representing the divine Shepherd of God's assembly or congregation. This is a book addressed to the people of God. It has a pastoral purpose. It is not addressed to unbelievers as an apologetic for the faith.

What we have here in the book we call Ecclesiastes is the apex of the wisdom of Solomon; not the pseudo-wisdom of a backslidden Solomon. This is the wisdom of Solomon as he occupies the office of shepherd of Israel—as he speaks for the Chief Shepherd.

What does the Pastor, the shepherd king, teach? Not what we might expect a pastor to preach to his congregation. It might be helpful to think about whether or not God's people today are finding real satisfaction in what answers and "wisdom" they expect from our pulpits. As one author and pastor has noted recently:

> I drive my car and listen to the Christian radio station; something my wife always tells me I should stop doing ("because it only gets you upset"). There I hear preacher after preacher be so absolutely sure of his bombproof answers and his foolproof *biblical* interpretations (in spite of the fact that Preacher A at 9:30 a.m. usually contradicts Preacher B at 10:00 a.m. and so on throughout the day), his five easy steps (alliterated around the letter *p*) . . . And the more sure he seems, the less I find myself wanting to be a Christian, because on this side of the microphone, antennas, and speakers, life isn't that simple, answers aren't that clear, and nothing is that sure. (Brian McLaren, *A New Kind of Christian* [San Francisco: Jossey-Bass, 2001], xiii)

Ecclesiastes is written by a different kind of pastor with a different kind of preaching.

THE PLAN OF ECCLESIASTES

Solomon doesn't show all his cards at once. He builds a case, he develops an argument, he progressively spirals in on his major themes. He targets them using "delightful words" which he describes as "well-driven nails" (Eccl. 12:11). The result is that if we follow him carefully, we too will partake of his Spirit-inspired wisdom.

This is why honoring Ecclesiastes with scattered slogans in our culture is not the best way to grasp its wisdom. The book is an argument. It makes up a coherent whole. It is not the compilation of various tidbits of loosely associated aphorisms all stuck together by some later author. Ecclesiastes is not meant to be parceled out into songs and sayings in popular culture. Solomon argues consistently and well for his conclusion: Christians will confess their ignorance and impotence and yet nevertheless receive and rejoice in everything God gives them in life, fearing him and keeping his commands.

The thematic cross-currents and swiftly-moving literary landscape have spoiled academic types of people into thinking that there are between four and nine different authors represented. They point out places within the book that appear to be contradictory, and to them this indicates multiple authors, but that is a superficial way of reading. They misunderstand the way Ecclesiastes works. The Spirit who inspired Ecclesiastes is the same Spirit who inspired four different gospel accounts to give us one gospel message. Solomon examines life from multiple perspectives and differing angles. Each time he reaches a tentative conclusion, he sums it up. The arrangement of the book is not accidental or haphazard. Rather, there is organic connection between the parts—a spiral-like progression that brings a satisfying conclusion for the man or woman of faith.

We find in Ecclesiastes four movements or sections, marked out for us by four conclusions:

1:2–2:26	There is nothing better for a person than that he should eat and drink and find enjoyment in his toil. This also, I saw, is from the hand of God, far apart from him who can eat or who can have enjoyment. For to the one who pleases him God has given wisdom and knowledge and joy, but to the sinner he has given the business of gathering and collecting, only to give to one who pleases God. This also is [vapor] and a striving after wind. (2:24–26)
3:1–5:20	Behold, what I have seen to be good and fitting is to eat and drink and find enjoyment in all the toil with which one toils under the sun the few days of his life that God has given him, for this is his lot. Everyone also to whom God has given wealth and possessions and power to enjoy them, and to accept his lot and rejoice in his toil—this is the gift of God. For he will not much remember the days of his life because God keeps him occupied with joy in his heart. (5:18–20)
6:1–8:15	And I commend joy, for man has no good thing under the sun but to eat and drink and be joyful, for this will go with him in his toil through the days of his life that God has given him under the sun. (8:15)
8:16–12:14	Besides being wise, the Preacher also taught the people knowledge, weighing and studying and arranging many proverbs with great care. The Preacher sought to find words of delight, and uprightly he wrote words of truth. The words of the wise are like goads, and like nails firmly fixed are the collected sayings; they are given by one Shepherd. My son, beware of anything beyond these. Of making many books there is no end, and much study is a weariness of the flesh. The end of the matter; all has been heard. Fear God and keep his commandments, for this is the whole duty of man. For God will bring every deed into judgment, with every secret thing, whether good or evil. (12:9–14)

I cannot simply state the conclusion for you. The purpose of Ecclesiastes can only be reached by *reading* it. I hope to help you read it, but there is no substitute for reading the book. It is like a poem. Poetry can be analyzed and summarized into certain basic themes or ideas a poet wants to convey, but to state the ideas in propositional form does *not* accurately reproduce the point of the poem. The words are supposed to change the reader in a way that cannot be duplicated by prose. Cognitive decoding may have its place, but it will not reach the poet's desired result. An analysis of a poem can help you understand it, but only if the poem itself is also read.

To understand Ecclesiastes, you have to go the whole way with Solomon through his writing, for he is not simply trying to state information, but to bring the reader to the point that he can actually grasp true wisdom. For that to happen, you must enter into his argument and into his experience. You must see in Ecclesiastes, mirrored for us, our own experiences as the people of God. You will also discern, as the argument of the book progresses, the fulfillment of Ecclesiastes in the life and teaching of Jesus, the greater Solomon. But I don't want to give away too much up front. At the end of the process you will have a better grasp of the truth. *Enjoy God's gifts of life while fearing him and keeping his commandments. God is in control. He will bring everything to a fitting and just conclusion. Faith will be satisfied with that.*

2

A Short Primer on Wisdom and Wisdom Literature

Give your servant therefore an understanding mind to govern your people, that I may discern between good and evil, for who is able to govern this your great people? —2 Kings 3:6

Before moving on to the text of Ecclesiastes, it may be helpful to step back for a moment and examine the function and character of wisdom literature in the Bible. The reader may want to skip this chapter and move directly to the exposition of Ecclesiastes, but I would advise against it. Getting the lay of the biblical-theological land will enrich your understanding of Solomon's words and help you appreciate the book's place in the story of Israel. Before I go hunting on unfamiliar land I like to look at a few maps of the surrounding area. Hastily-drawn directions to the deer stand are not enough. I want to know where the creeks, roads, hills, valleys, fields, barns, and homes are located before I even think about shooting. A map of the area will also help me discern what to expect when I arrive. Where will the deer likely be coming from? Where are the best spots for a tree stand? Similarly, although one might read Ecclesiastes without knowing where it fits into the larger map of Old Testament literature, a short look at the flow of biblical history and Ecclesiastes' place in that history will go a long way toward orienting you to receive Solomon's intended instruction. If you are looking to bag some wisdom, you best know where it comes from and what it might look like.

THE ODDNESS OF WISDOM LITERATURE

> I have counsel and sound wisdom;
>   I have insight; I have strength.
> By me kings reign,
>   and rulers decree what is just;
> by me princes rule,
>   and nobles, all who govern justly.
> I love those who love me,
>   and those who seek me diligently find me. (Prov. 8:14–17)

"By me kings reign." This is wisdom speaking. Those who would rule as kings need wisdom to do so effectively. The wisdom literature of the Bible was written for this purpose. The book of Proverbs, for example, was written by a king for a prince (by Solomon for his son, the future king): "The proverbs of Solomon, son of David, king of Israel: to know wisdom. . . . Listen, my son, to your father's instruction" (Prov. 1:1–2a, 8). Ecclesiastes is also written by King Solomon for the same end: "I the Shepherd have been king over Israel in Jerusalem, and I applied by heart to seek and search out by wisdom all that is done under heaven" (Eccl. 1:12; cf. 1:1). Although not as obvious at first glance, the same is true for the Song of Songs. It, too, was written "by Solomon" (Song 1:1; 8:11); and although the word "wisdom" does not occur in the book itself, Luther wisely discerned that the book is about the passionate love that ought to exist between a wise king and his subjects. Even the book of Job has to do with a tragedy that befell an ancient wise ruler by the same name (Job 29:1–25) and was probably written during the kingdom of David and Solomon. The man who would be king will learn wisdom by reading and meditating on all of these books.

These, then, are the books (including a few of the psalms) commonly designated as "wisdom literature." They are written by kings for kings. They intend to instruct us in royal wisdom. That being said, a modern person might therefore expect to find a manual on how to administer a kingdom. We might even expect something very "practical"—advice about how to choose suitable advisors, rules that might help monarchs effectively lead an army, or sound principles and guidelines necessary in order to manage a kingdom's complex finances, but this is *not* what we get.

American Christians often read wisdom literature anticipating concrete, functional advice. Ask an American what wisdom is and you are likely to get an answer that has to do with practical know-how. You will be told that a wise man knows more than *theory*; he knows *how* to do things. A wise man, therefore, will be able to figure things out. More than that, he'll be able to *fix* things. So wisdom is the ability to figure things out and the practical skill to get things done—to control one's life and circumstances.

With these presuppositions, we think we already know what kind of information and knowledge a king might need to rule his realm, but when we actually read these royal wisdom books, we are a bit surprised, possibly even disappointed. It is comparable to the disappointment a man might experience if he were to walk into his local hardware store and discover that they did not stock hammers, drill bits, screws, nails, wood, or anything else that might help him fix his broken shed. Apparently, however, royal wisdom cannot be equated with the nitty-gritty details of how to manage one's realm. Wisdom literature does not communicate *that* kind of practical knowledge. It is this surprise—this oddness of the content of wisdom (at least to us Americans)—that we need to explore a little before we wade into the book of Ecclesiastes.

In order to understand the oddness of wisdom literature, it is necessary for us to appreciate the timing of the writing of these books in the history of Israel. Far from being unimportant, the fact that these wisdom books show up in connection with the kingdom phase of Israel's history is enormously significant.

We modern Christians are often tempted to flatten the Bible out and treat it as a compilation of proof texts for building up a timeless systematic theology or as a collection of exemplary stories about moral character or conversion experiences. Unfortunately, too many preachers and teachers use the Bible in this way. As we shall see, however, if we give careful attention to where the Bible situates wisdom in the story of man, this will help us come to some understanding of the meaning of biblical wisdom.

THE STORY OF ISRAEL-PRIESTHOOD

Before we go all the way back to Adam and Eve and the beginning of the story—a move we must make eventually if we are to appreciate wisdom's role in mankind's progress toward maturity—let us begin with something fairly straightforward and easy to see. Think about the narrative of Israel's history. There are at least three fairly obvious stages in Israel's development. Think of these as stages in God's process of educating or training his people. This is one of the ways Paul encourages us to meditate on the story of God's interaction with his people Israel in the old world (Gal. 4:1–7). They were being trained or educated as God's new humanity. The three stages can be outlined as follows:

Priests ⟶ Kings ⟶ Prophets

This ordered sequence is important. As a nation covenanted to Yahweh, Israel begins her corporate life as priests. What we call the Mosaic covenant, which Yahweh graciously inaugurates with Israel at Mount Sinai, is largely concerned with regulating his people's priestly role in the world at large. A "priest" is a household servant of Yahweh. Israel is granted the privilege of drawing near to God and therefore of serving in his house (the tabernacle). I hardly need to amass proof texts to demonstrate that the Mosaic covenant and the revelation associated with that covenant largely concerns priestly and sacrificial regulations.

At this stage in the story of Israel, she is charged with guarding and maintaining the Lord's special "house." She is granted this charge to serve the nations. What we call the tabernacle is Yahweh's special "tent of meeting," the appointed place to which he invites his people to draw near and commune with him. This meeting place is a place of food and feasting, which is why so much of the content of the Mosaic regulations have to do with clean and unclean foods, animals that are appropriate for Yahweh's food, and the appointed times and places for such festival banquets.

As the Lord's priests, his people serve as inspectors and servants at his communion Table (what we call the "altar"). The special priests (Levites and the sons of Aaron) inspect, prepare, and distribute the Lord's food. I wish that our translations would make this more clear. Every animal that is brought near (the Hebrew verb is *qrb*, "to draw near") becomes "food" (*lechem*, "bread") for God. Speaking to the Aaronic priests in Leviticus 21:6, Yahweh says "They shall be holy to their God and not profane the name of their God. For they bring near (*qrb*) Yahweh's fire-cooked food (*'isheh*), the bread (*lechem*) of their God."

Much more could be said, of course, but this is enough to get the general thrust of Israel's priestly duties. What we must pay careful attention to now is that priestly regulations are very detailed and do not require a great deal of discernment to administer. The Law (Torah) is quite meticulous. To be faithful priests, Israel simply had to follow the Law very carefully. If an animal is brought near for the Lord's Table, the priests simply had to remember God's explicit instruction and discern whether an animal was clean and unclean, blemished or unblemished, and so on.

So much of what we call "the Law" or "the Torah" is like this: do this, do that, do not do this, and do not do that. Israel began her corporate life with relatively simple, straightforward rules to follow. The same is true for the laws that regulated her social and governmental existence. Of course, it is true that for us modern readers this legal system often seems hopelessly complex, but that is only because we are so far removed from the life of Israel and the old world of animal sacrifices. As others have pointed out, however, for an Israelite to acquire expertise in these matters was not much different than the way a car mechanic today learns the "rules" that govern the replacement and repair of auto parts. Most of us would be lost until we spent the necessary hours memorizing the parts manuals for this kind of work, and the laws governing animal sacrifice are a lot simpler than those that apply to modern car maintenance and repair.

My point is this: Israel began her life in Yahweh's house learning the rules explicitly laid out by him for her priestly duties. She was like a child who is governed by specific "dos and don'ts" unmistakably expressed by her parents. She began in God's house serving at his Table. All of this is not to deny that there are "deeper" dimensions to the Mosaic Law. There certainly are. We will get to that in a moment, but for now, simply notice that Israel's early relation to God was very childlike. She was called to obey even if she didn't fully understand. She needed to mature as she obeyed God's Law in order to appropriate the "wisdom" embodied in the Law.

Back to the Garden

Before we move on to the next phase of Israel's story, we should stop and return to the beginning of human history. Since we are reflecting on biblical wisdom and are about to embark on a study of the wisdom of Solomon expressed in Ecclesiastes, it would be helpful for us to go back to the "book of beginnings" and think about the way in which wisdom is first presented to us. The Hebrew word "wisdom" does not itself occur in the story of Adam and Eve in Genesis 1–3, but it is clear from the details of the story that God promised kingly wisdom to Adam if he would be patient and wait for God to mature him.

The promise of royal wisdom which God held out to Adam was embodied in the Tree of the Knowledge of Good and Evil. This perspective is not often appreciated, but a little investigation into how the Bible later uses the notion of the "knowledge of good and evil" reveals that it is the wise discernment exercised by those placed in positions of authority and responsibility. Knowing or discerning between good and evil has to do with making mature judgments. It is a precious gift of God sought by those called to rule. Those given the gift to discern good and evil possess the wisdom necessary for deciding life and death issues for those whom they serve as rulers. The woman of Tekoa recognizes that King David was a "messenger of God to discern good and evil" (2 Sam. 14:17). Indeed, David was able to unravel in this story a very convoluted situation that ultimately concerns the life and death of his son Absalom.

The best illustration of the meaning of "knowing good and evil" is found in the story of young Solomon's prayer for wisdom. Realizing that he is too young to have the weight of the kingdom on his shoulders, Solomon petitions God for the wisdom he needs to rule. He is not presumptuous like Adam. He does not prematurely seize power. Rather, when given the opportunity to ask anything of the Lord, Solomon makes this request:

> And now, O Lord my God, you have made your servant king in place of David my father, although I am but a little child. I do not know how to go out or come in. And your servant is in the midst of your people whom you have chosen, a great people, too many to be numbered or counted for multitude. Give your servant therefore an understanding mind to govern your people, that I may discern between good and evil, for who is able to govern this your great people? (1 Kings 3:7–9)

God commends Solomon for his appropriate request and gifts him with "a wise and discerning mind." Solomon, the son of David, is a new Adam. The text of 1 Kings calls attention to this shortly after Solomon's prayer for wisdom, recounting his Adamic accomplishments (1 Kings 4:29–34).

Children do not know "good and evil" in this judicial sense (Deut. 1:39), which is why elders—not young people—are given the privilege of adjudicating cases in the community. Even though Adam and Eve began their biological life as adults, they were nonetheless children in their experience of life and the world. It seems evident that God's program for them was to gain wisdom through their experience of life and the world, patiently waiting for God to grant them the gift of royal judicial authority symbolized by the Tree of the Knowledge of Good and Evil. As Adam faithfully ate of the Tree of Life, giving thanks to God for his life, and as he diligently guarded and served the Garden of Eden and his new wife situated in the midst of the Garden, he would slowly mature into the kind of man qualified to rule over God's creation. That was the plan, anyway.

The tragedy recorded for us in Genesis 3, however, is that Adam failed to guard the Garden and his new bride from the attack of the Serpent. They seized what God had asked them to wait for and as a result they were banished from the Garden. With fatal consequences, Adam presumptuously and prematurely snatched what would have been his if he had trusted God's promise—the authority to judge good and evil. He listened to the Serpent and decided that he didn't want to wait for God's permission to rule. The seductive power of being "like God" now and ruling like him, "judging good and evil," overcame our original parents.

God's plan, however, was not thereby thwarted. God's program for the maturation of humanity continued. Now, however, after the fall, mankind would learn and grow into a mature image of God only through intense suffering and the curse of death. But the path to maturity, although now more difficult and frustrating, was nevertheless the same. Whether it was Abraham and his descendents or Israel herself, they experienced life first as priests (guarding and serving the worship of God) and then were graciously given the privilege of "discerning good and evil" as kings. Abraham and his altars gave way to Jacob ruling over his large family and finally Joseph's wise administration of the entire world in Egypt. From priesthood to kingship—that is the initial flow of God's program of maturity for his people.

Just as God intended Adam and Abraham's family to mature from priest to priest-king, so also the kingdom was envisioned in the priestly Law for Israel (Deut. 17:14–20). As the Lord's new humanity (new Adam), Israel was to patiently wait for the Lord to bestow the responsibility of kingship on them when they were ready. If they would faithfully guard God's house and serve at the Table in his house, they would grow in wisdom and eventually mature into a nation capable of the larger responsibility of kingship. Israel began with service at the altar and tabernacle of God until she was ready to administer the kingdom some five hundred years later. When David and Solomon ruled, they also wrote. The Law was given through Moses, but psalms and wisdom literature came through David and his son.

This has been a rough and ready summary of the story of mankind and Israel from the perspective of their maturation from priesthood to kingship. A great deal more could be said. We have not even discussed the prophetic climax of maturity. Since the prophetic stage of the story is not directly germane to the study of the book of Ecclesiastes, I'll only point out that becoming a prophet means even greater responsibility and authority. Contrary to popular notions, prophets are not merely God's errand boys, simply delivering messages they hear in the heavenly court. Rather, prophets have been elevated to the rank of advisor and council member. God allows them to participate in the heavenly court's deliberation before he makes a decision to act (Amos 3:7; 7:1–9). The prophet's words, then, have a power beyond that of kings (Jer. 1:9–10). They have the ear of the Almighty. When they speak, history changes; nations are alternately delivered or uprooted and destroyed.

This, then, is the basic outline of the story of humanity's maturation according to God's own pedagogy. We see it in the story of Abraham and his family as well as in the story of Israel as a whole:

Priest (Abraham) ⟶ King (Jacob) ⟶ Prophet (Joseph)

Note how the story of the Bible begins with priests who have a limited service in God's sanctuary, then progresses so that the priests become kings who rule in their own land, and finally ends with a flurry of prophetic activity relating to the whole of world history. It begins with priestly service in the sanctuary (Mosaic), followed by kingly rule in the land (David & sons), and finally prophetic advisors who change the world (Daniel).

The education and maturity of humanity would culminate in God the Son assuming our human nature and living as a man among us. Jesus, the last Adam, would not fail to serve and guard his bride, the church. He is flawlessly faithful in his priestly service. Indeed, Jesus did not grasp for kingship as Adam did, but allowed God to bestow it upon him (Phil. 2:5–11). He did what Adam would not do. He refused the Serpent's temptation to seize prematurely what his father had promised him (Matt. 4:1–11). Jesus knew that the path to wisdom was learning maturity through suffering (Heb. 5:8). The writer of Hebrews tells us that "being made mature," Jesus was granted the Davidic promise to sit down at the father's right hand (Heb. 1; Ps. 2, 110).

WISDOM LITERATURE AND ECCLESIASTES

All of this is important background for understanding the wisdom literature of the Old Testament. We noted earlier that Israel was given rather straightforward directions in the Mosaic Law. She was also promised abundant blessing when she obeyed the Law and frightening curses if she chose to transgress God's covenantal stipulations (Deut. 27–29). This, too, corresponds with how children learn. For example, a little boy learns that it is wrong to do something that puts a sibling or friend in danger of harm. "Don't do that!" the parent commands. But when the boy grows up and is put in a place of leadership, for example, in the military, he will discover that it is often necessary to send some of his men on dangerous, sometimes fatal, missions, in order to accomplish a greater goal. The wisdom literature of the Bible recognizes that ruling involves wise discernment and decisive action in life-and-death situations. After asking for and receiving wisdom from God, Solomon's first dilemma called for him to decree death to the infant son claimed by both prostitutes (1 Kings 4:16–28). The decree was not carried out, of course. On the face of it, for a king to command such a thing seems to violate the Law of God, and yet it was the wisest thing to do in that situation.

As Israel matured and began to reflect upon the complexities of life and the challenges of ruling a nation, she discerned that everything is not so black and white, and that God does not simply reward obedience with material blessings and disobedience with poverty and calamity. No, life is more complex than that and God's ways are often quite paradoxical because his explicit intentions are not available to us.

The riddle character of life is reflected in the use of riddles in the wise man's reflection on the world and life. Solomon's explanation of the purpose of his proverbs includes a summons to the wise: "Let the wise hear and increase in learning, and the one who understands obtain guidance, to understand a proverb and a dark saying, the words of the wise and their riddles" (Prov. 1:5–6). The word "proverb" translates the Hebrew word *maschal*, which is a rather broad term that is used to describe short, pithy, riddle-like sayings (what we call "proverbs") as well as longer, more complex stories—what we might call "parables." In every case, however, this *maschal* literature of the wise has an enigmatic dimension to it. The meaning lies beneath the surface. The fool, who only looks at the superficial, surface meaning, will not understand. One must be wise to understand the sayings of the wise; or maybe better, if one diligently ponders and searches for the meaning of these dark sayings, one will attain wisdom (Prov. 2:1–9).

This means that the dominant literary mode of expressing the reflections of the wisdom teachers requires more than a superficial reading. Riddles take time and effort to solve. Unfortunately, some who comment on Ecclesiastes don't move beyond a superficial reading and conclude that Solomon has become despondent and given up on life, or that he has written what amounts to an exposé of the unbeliever's perspective on the world. This is a failure of the imagination. Such an interpretation may also say more about the interpreter than the text. A wise man will resonate to Solomon's frustration with the ephemeral character of life under the sun. The superficially pious man calls for positive attitudes and cheery one-dimensional slogans about life and the world, but the wise man knows better. He has experienced Solomon's theme: "Everything is vapor." And armed with this, therefore, the wise man is ready by faith to rule the world.

Part One

Ecclesiastes 1:2–2:26

3

Everything is Vapor: Ecclesiastes 1:2–11

What is your life? For you are a vapor that appears for a little time and then vanishes. —James 4:14b

Natural disasters strike so seldom, and our technological achievements are so great, that we occasionally see signs that people are entirely forgetting who they are and where they stand. When I was first preparing to preach on Ecclesiastes, the news was filled with stories of how tornadoes and storms had laid waste to several counties in Florida. One local government official in Florida was asked by a news reporter, "What would you have done differently to help avoid this disaster?" He responded with irritation. He was visibly annoyed. "What could we have done differently? This was an act of God! How could we have controlled the outcome?" Wise answer.

Twenty-first-century man, however, is not often so wise. He is obsessed with control. We are all control freaks. We think that life can be programmed like a computer—that all we need is the right technique. If we just find the proper method we will have control. This is true in government, science, and social work. It is the quest we pursue in our families and other relationships. The search for the power—the hunt for control over our destinies—never ends.

Congress thinks it can engineer a certain type of society. Our judges no longer adjudicate right and wrong based on objective standards; they are social engineers looking toward the proper effects of a law. It was only a few years ago I saw a prominent national politician actually shaking his fist at El Niño, the disruptive wind in the tropical Pacific that causes heavy weather and alters the climate around the globe. *We will fight and win! We will defeat El Niño.* Whatever his exact words, that was the gist of it. *We are the U.S. of A, by golly! We have computers and satellites and airplanes and weather instruments. We can pass laws!*

At root, this is pagan. It is a pagan drive to find the secret that will allow man to manipulate reality to his advantage. All the temples, sacrifices, oracles, Ouija boards, witches' brews, and incantations in the ancient word were fallen man's arrogant attempt to leverage nature. A magic talisman or secret-power words are desired that will unlock creation's secrets and give a man or woman power over the natural world. The unlocking of this secret is inappropriately described as "wisdom."

It is great fun to take a young child for his first visit to the ocean beach and introduce him to the fun of sandcastles. Children love constructing castles, walls, towers, and moats. They are usually enthralled with the process and thrilled with the results, but it is easy for a parent to fail to prepare a child for the nature of sandcastle-building on the beach. Inevitably the tide comes in, the moat fills up, and the sweeping waves dissolve everything the child has worked for. Adults expect this. They are not disappointed and they don't try to change the way things are. Maturity, in this case, means understanding the limits of sand sculpting. Young children have to learn this through experience. At first, like those reporters asking how the disaster could have been avoided, they want to think there must be some way to stop the tide and the wind and make the sandcastles last.

Many who read this passage might assume that Solomon is saying that all the cycles of nature are "vapor." That is not his point. In verse three he asks a question that tells us what he means: "What does man *gain* by all the toil at which he toils under the sun?" Everything we do is like the building of a sandcastle, he is saying. Nature is impervious to all our work.

In the poem that flows from verse two to verse eleven, Solomon makes his first attempt to remind us how severely limited we are as human creatures. The poem unpacks the ephemeral nature of man's endeavors. We don't make things happen. Things happen over and over again no matter what we do. We can't change them. They change us. We are moved *from* life by forces that are just as much outside our control as were the forces that brought us *into* life. Our sandcastles never last. Listen to the wisdom of Solomon in the opening words of Ecclesiastes:

> [Vapor] of [vapors], says the Preacher,
> [Vapor] of [vapors]! All is [vapor].
> What does man gain by all the toil
> at which he toils under the sun?
> A generation goes, and a generation comes,
> but the earth remains forever.
> The sun rises, and the sun goes down,
> and hastens to the place where it rises.
> The wind blows to the south
> and goes around to the north;
> around and around goes the wind,
> and on its circuits the wind returns.
> All streams run to the sea,
> but the sea is not full;
> to the place where the streams flow,
> there they flow again. (1:2–7)

This passage is not a romantic poem about the rich, limitless variety of creation. It is not a celebration of all the exotic wonders of the world God made. There are other portions of Scripture that do just that. Rather, these stanzas epitomize the futility of man's efforts over against a world order that does not yield to his influence. Like the bunny in the battery commercials, nature keeps going and going and going, without regard for man's work. These verses about creation portray the insubstantial nature of human activity.

The phrase "under the sun" is a quiet hint up front, and occurs at least thirty times in the book. It declares the perspective from which everything is only "vapor"—the place of man. The world that man can observe and the world that man seeks to influence and control is under the sun. It is our ground-level observation point from which we try to make the world work for us—to find a leverage point in the confusing whirl we call life. Though one may attempt such things, if one is wise—truly wise—and if one believes in God, then it will all be recognizable as vapor.

I need to explain why I have used the word "vapor" in the preceding two paragraphs. This is crucial to understanding the book as a whole. The noun traditionally translated "vanity" (KJV, ESV) and in many modern versions "meaninglessness" (NIV) is the Hebrew word *hebel*. This word is used in many places to refer to a wisp, a vapor, a puff of air that disappears, a mere breath (e.g., Prov. 21:6). Indeed, pagan idols are sometimes designated as *hebel* because they are so insubstantial and light (e.g., Jer. 10:15). Whatever the connotative significance of the use of the vapor metaphor might be in any given passage, the word denotes a "mist" or "vapor." That raw image ought to be made clear in our translations.

Solomon uses this word *hebel* no fewer than thirty-five times in Ecclesiastes. The repetition "*hebel* of *hebels*" is an idiomatic expression for the superlative. It is like the reference to the inner chamber of the temple as the "Holy of Holies." Or think of how we call Jesus the "King of kings and Lord of lords." "Vapor of vapors," then, refers to the supreme vapor, the ultimate wisp. The world and life is a wisp. It is the dust particle drifting in the sunbeam. It escapes your efforts when you attempt to attain it. You cannot catch it. It eludes your grasp. When you try to snatch it and hold it, it always slips out of your hand.

Unfortunately, rather than a literal translation of the word, many Bible versions interpret *hebel* as either "vanity" or "meaningless." In my view both of these are inaccurate and introduce confusion into the text. First, the word "vanity" implies a moral judgment and often makes us think of Vanity Fair from *Pilgrim's Progress*, a depraved carnival where people indulge in vain, immoral frivolities. A vain person is someone who is conceited, someone concerned with appearances. A vanity is a mirrored desk where you sit and pretty yourself up. None of these associations helps us understand the meaning of *hebel*. When Solomon says "all is *hebel*" he is not saying that everything is conceited, vain, or vacuous. Our word "vanity" derives from the Latin *vanitas*, which means "empty," but all of life is *not* empty, nor is the world empty. Actually, life is quite full. Man's work is not "vanity." As we shall see, Solomon commends labor or work to the one who trusts God.

"Meaningless" is probably a worse translation than "vanity." Life is not meaningless. Man's work is not meaningless. That is the last thing that Solomon wants to convey. "Meaningless" does not catch the essence of *hebel*. One modern Christian author, commenting on the significance of Ecclesiastes, tells us that the book was written to convince the unbeliever of the meaninglessness of his life. "There is an alternative to meaninglessness. It is to see the world God's way." If *hebel* meant "meaningless," then this would be the only real option for understanding Ecclesiastes, but *hebel* is not primarily a negative evaluation of the ultimate rationality or meaningfulness of the cosmos, either in itself, or in a life lived in alienation from God. Everything is *not* meaningless. Rather, as we shall see, everything eludes our grasp and defies our attempts at comprehension and control. Everything is smoke, mist, vapor.

The point is that there is no advantage or ultimate leverage in our work. The universe marches on just like the waves on the beach. Our labor always meets the fate of the sandcastles. Solomon asks what "gain" or "profit" can be found in our labor (Eccl. 1:3). The Hebrew word he uses (*yithron*) refers to gaining "leverage" in the world—some sort of advantage. It is futile to think that man can leverage the world and life by means of his own labor and toil.

Vapor describes all of man's activity, his pursuit of and enjoyment of pleasure, his acquisition of property, and his growth in knowledge or wealth. Vapor, for example, is a fitting metaphor for "natural advantages" some have, such as youthfulness or physical strength. It is all *hebel.*

It is interesting that the Hebrew word *hebel* is used in a prominent story early in the Bible. The name "Abel" is the English transliteration for the Hebrew *hebel.* Abel, Adam and Eve's second son, became the first recorded death in Scripture and the first recorded murder victim. His ungodly older brother, Cain, killed him out of jealousy.

Think of how Adam and Eve must have rejoiced in their children. Adam and Eve fell into sin and were thrust from the Garden of Eden because Adam wanted to take control of his life and grab wisdom. Now, at least, with the birth of these sons, Adam and Eve would have some comfort. Perhaps they could now restore some meaning and purpose in their lives after being banished from the Garden. Cain's naming has long teased Christian commentators because it looks as if Eve expected her son to be the promised seed who would crush the serpent's head (Gen. 3:15; 4:1). After years of building up such misplaced hopes, suddenly they find Cain is a killer rather than a savior, and that Abel's life has ended for no good reason at all. Cain is banished and Abel is lifeless. Imagine Adam and Eve's response to the death of their son, the first human death they ever experience. *Why? How? Where is my son? What could we have done?* Who first found Abel's lifeless body? Who had to pick it up? *So this is what physical death is! Lifelessness. An empty shell of a body, useless and futile, incomprehensible. For what purpose? To what end? Why?*

There is a real question as to whether Adam or Eve named Abel at birth or if that name was given to him later. Unlike Cain, nothing is said about how or when Abel was named by his parents. The narrator simply declares that Cain's brother was *vapor,* a breath. Perhaps the name was given after his sudden death. Whatever name the boy had upon birth was utterly forgotten; from now on he would be remembered as *Hebel.*

Or else perhaps Abel originally meant something else. Perhaps the Hebrew word gained its very meaning from the premature and unexpected death of Abel. Either way, *Hebel's* death was a concrete instance of man's tragic plight and a sobering wake-up call to Adam and Eve. Life is a vapor. A wisp. Things were out of their control. Even their own son's life and death was so utterly outside of their ability to control that they could not even explain it. It made no sense to them. It appeared absurd, pointless, useless, without reason. It never had to be. How should they respond to such an event? What could they do when confronted with such a revelation of the nature of their now post-fall world? There were only two options for them. They could jettison their trust in the goodness and love of God or they could jettison all hope of comprehending and controlling the world and more completely place their faith in God.

Abel (*hebel*) now became indicative of life "under the sun." Life under the sun for humanity is the supreme Abel, *hebel* of *hebels*. Adam and Eve, of course, did not quit life. They did not abandon their faith. They moved on, in spite of *hebel*, even though *everything* is *hebel* to them, everything vaporous and unmanageable, utterly out of their control and comprehension. The Lord did not give them a tour of his cosmic control tower. They remained on ground level, under the sun where everything was *hebel*.

All that remained was for them to trust in God. When everything is *hebel*, the only thing left is faith in the Lord, the covenant-keeping, promise-honoring God. Adam learned the lesson of faith, of trust. Eve did, too. So did Enoch, Noah, Abraham, Isaac, Jacob, Joseph, Moses, Joshua, Samuel, David, and the wise King Solomon. How about you?

WHAT'S NEW?

"Five minutes of fame." "Everyone wants to be a star." Our media-centered culture's slogans manifest both the wisdom of Ecclesiastes and the foolishness with which most of us delude ourselves. People seem to think life is not worth living unless they can be famous. Reality television and the increasing number of contest shows give many people the idea that they too can and should get their time in front of the camera. This is strongly desired as some sort of great reward even when everyone acknowledges that it is not very rewarding. Not only is fame not all that important, but it almost never lasts. Even when someone manages to get invited on the *Tonight Show*, it is very unlikely that he will make it to a second invitation. Anyone who has worked and strained to get their five minutes of fame will find they must work all the harder to make it last ten minutes.

People forget. The person who sang the best during the last television season will not be remembered as an idol during this season because the public wants someone new. Even famous movie stars are eventually forgotten by a new generation. Inevitably, they become known long enough to interest the Biography Channel and soon after that, they are gone. After all, there have been many people on television and in the movies and there still are. Stars come and go. People are always questing for what comes next so that invariably they forget last year's celebrity.

Eventually, everything is forgotten. Just ask a child where the term "dial tone" came from, or why we say some people "sound like a broken record." Meditate on King Solomon's lament in Ecclesiastes 1:8–11:

> All things are full of weariness;
>   a man cannot utter it;
> the eye is not satisfied with seeing,
>   nor the ear filled with hearing.
> What has been is what will be,
>   and what has been done is what will be done,
>   and there is nothing new under the sun.
> Is there a thing of which it is said,
>   "See, this is new"?
> It has been already
>   in the ages before us.
> There is no remembrance of former things,
>   nor will there be any remembrance
> of later things yet to be
>   among those who come after.

In this latter part of Solomon's initial poem, the unending march of nature, which he has described so vividly, gives way to the significance of the unending succession of generations. Solomon does not merely describe the boredom of humanity, but also points out how utterly limited man is. Human beings can only do what they have been given to do by God. Everything man achieves falls into certain categories which really do not change.

Suppose you could bring Solomon forward in time to your own day. Imagine trying to say, "Look, Solomon, at all the new things that we twentieth-century humans have produced!"

He says, "Where?"

"Over there! That Frank Lloyd Wright architectural masterpiece." Solomon says, "It's a building; people have been making buildings for the last six millennia."

"Well," you say, "read this great novel. No one has ever written anything like it." "Fine," Solomon says, "it's a book, a story. What's new about that? Show me something *new*."

"Okay, then, how about this jet plane? Look at that technology. That's new."

"Yeah!" Solomon says, "I acknowledge the newness of these technologies, but what does air travel do? It's a form of transportation. So you get there faster. Big whoop! It's the same old problem. Man has to get from point A to point B."

"Okay, I've got you now. Look at this thing here. You never had anything like this before. We call it a computer."

"What does it do?" Solomon asks.

"You can write more efficiently with it, calculate numbers, communicate, and organize your life."

"Yeah," Solomon says, "man's been trying to do those things more efficiently all through his history. What's new about that? Does it guarantee efficiency? Does it make a man write better? Does it insure accurate calculations?"

"Well, no. Garbage in, garbage out."

"Exactly," Solomon says. "There's nothing new. By the way," he asks, "what about this icon here?"

"That's my web browser," you answer.

"What does that do?"

"It makes rapid communication possible."

"Sounds interesting. Has it changed our lives for the better?"

"Not really, no," you admit.

That there is nothing new under the sun does not mean that man does not invent, that he does not genuinely reflect his Creator by building and making wonderful new things. But after all, what is really new? Man does what he's done since the dawn of time. He works, builds, barters, eats, drinks, walks, sleeps, and dies. What leverage do these activities give mankind?

What advantage will you accrue from your exhausting labor? Will you make a name for yourself? Maybe, but for how long? "There is no remembrance of former things, nor will there be any remembrance of later things yet to be among those who come after" (Eccl. 1:11). The Pastor reminds us of the ceaseless making and unmaking that goes on in human history. "The paths of glory," the English poet Thomas Gray observed, "lead but to the grave." Wave after wave, the rise and fall of generations and nations goes on and on. All of this takes place against the background of a cosmos that is God's creation and not ours—a cosmos that does not seem to be affected.

Those are the facts. All of man's feverish activity and labor is *hebel*. Vapor. What does he accomplish? What advantage does it bring to us? In all of man's work and labor, he changes nothing, he controls nothing, he successfully manipulates nothing that matters. Everything goes on the same as it has because everything is outside of our control! Unbelievers do not accept this fact, but faithful Christians who have acquired wisdom know that it is true. And they trust God and enjoy life just the same.

4

Learning from Solomon's Quest: Ecclesiastes 1:12–2:26

Aspire to live quietly, and to mind your own affairs, and to work with your hands, as we instructed you. —1 Thessalonians 4:11

Unless you've sealed yourself off from the world of police fiction in novels, television, and movies, you know exactly what I mean when I mention the strategy "good cop, bad cop." Two detective partners go into the room to elicit a confession from a suspect. They want to convict him by getting him to admit the truth. To do that, the two cops each play a role: one is overtly hostile and the other appears sympathetic and protective. The "good cop" might wait until the other officer is gone from the room for a moment (as they planned beforehand) and then secretly offer advice to the suspect that the only way to satisfy him is to confess the truth.

The royal shepherd of Ecclesiastes is like that good cop. He is whispering to us that it is no good trying to stonewall the bad cop;

we might as well give up and make a confession. The bad cop is the real nature of life "under the sun." The frustration caused by the fact that our labor and toil is useless for gaining real leverage—that it is fleeting and vaporous—is supposed to make us turn to God. The good news is that while the bad cop is trying to get us to confess, he is doing so not to condemn us but to save us.

Solomon gave an initial poetic evaluation in the previous verses. As we have seen, he evaluates all of humanity's endeavors to master life, to gain leverage over creation to his favor, as ultimately futile. They are *hebel*, vapor. Man's place in the world is severely circumscribed. He is created, dependent, and limited in space and time.

Perhaps we are in danger of looking at things too superficially. Maybe there is some advantage, some leverage that man can achieve by his labors "under the sun." *Let's see*, the Convener (*qoheleth*) says. *Follow me and join me on this quest.* Solomon now moves on and records his own attempt to answer the question of the advantage or profit of human labor and work. What ought we to do? What is our proper lot in this whirl of history and nature? Listen to Solomon describe our trouble in 1:12–18:

> I the Preacher have been king over Israel in Jerusalem. And I applied my heart to seek and to search out by wisdom all that is done under heaven. It is an unhappy business that God has given to the children of man to be busy with. I have seen everything that is done under the sun, and behold, all is [vapor] and [shepherding the wind].
>
> What is crooked cannot be made straight,
> and what is lacking cannot be counted.
>
> I said in my heart, "I have acquired great wisdom, surpassing all who were over Jerusalem before me, and my heart has had great experience of wisdom and knowledge." And I applied my heart to know wisdom and to know madness and folly. I perceived that this also is but [shepherding the wind].
>
> For in much wisdom is much vexation,
> and he who increases knowledge increases sorrow.

Bible scholar Robert K. Johnston observes: "Qoheleth's intent in his writing is to pass judgment on man's misguided endeavors at mastering life by pointing out its limits and mysteries. He would prefer that man replace such false and illusory hopes with a confidence based in the joy of creation as God's gift." This is not a very popular notion. Johnston gave his essay the apt name "Confessions of a Workaholic" (*Catholic Biblical Quarterly* 1976, 26).

What does God say to a nation of control freaks and workaholics? Typical of God, he asks us a searching question (compare Gen. 3:9, 11, 13; 4:6; Judg. 2:2): "What does man gain by all the toil at which he toils under the sun?" (Eccl. 1:3).

Here's that Hebrew word *yithron* again. We called attention to it briefly in commenting on 1:3. It is used ten times in Ecclesiastes at key junctures in the argument. It may be translated "profit," "gain," "advantage," or even "leverage." The root idea is that of surplus. Solomon asks us if man gets anything extra for his work. Does his working achieve for him some profit or gain that gives him leverage over life and its problems? No. There is no treasury of surplus power that we build up by working hard, no merit that we can use to leverage God and the world. When we have done all, "we are *unprofitable* servants, we have only done our duty" (Luke 17:10). With this in mind, one can easily see that Ecclesiastes has special relevance to us post-modern people who are franticly driven to master the world and life.

Furthermore, as Solomon tells us here in this passage, there is more to our problem than simply the inevitable cycles of nature and the generations. Men and women are not simply finite, but they are also sinful. Humanity is not only limited by its creaturely dependence, but is actually cursed by God. God has laid a heavy burden on men and women, a burden that is his own doing: he has twisted the world and it cannot be untwisted (Eccl. 1:13b–15; compare 7:13, 14).

Solomon's reference to what is twisted unquestionably refers to God's curse on humanity when Adam and Eve sinned. "It is an unhappy business that God has given to the children of man to be busy with" (1:13). God has laid upon man a "burdensome task," a "work of affliction," or a "painful business." The Hebrew could even be translated as an "evil task." The "children of men," as the ESV translates it, are actually *the sons of Adam* in Hebrew. The language Solomon uses harkens back to Genesis 3:17 and the Lord's judgment on Adam:

> Because you have listened to the voice of your wife
>   and have eaten of the tree
> of which I commanded you,
>   "You shall not eat of it,"
> cursed is the ground because of you;
>   in pain you shall eat of it all the days of your life;
> thorns and thistles it shall bring forth for you;
>   and you shall eat the plants of the field.
> By the sweat of your face
>   you shall eat bread,
> till you return to the ground,
>   for out of it you were taken;
> for you are dust,
>   and to dust you shall return.

God has laid a curse upon us. We are not merely described as creatures, but as creatures who have been laid upon, burdened! The whole created cosmos turned against Adam and Eve to frustrate them, to work against their work. This is the "work of affliction" which God has laid upon humanity in the post-fall world. This is yet another reason why verse fourteen says that all the works that are done under the sun are *hebel* and our attempts to control our lives by our own actions are an exercise in "shepherding the wind." The Hebrew verb used in this last phrase actually refers to "herding." Adam and Eve were given dominion over the creatures and were to shepherd them. They were not satisfied with this kingdom and thought they could attain an advantage by gaining wisdom and a greater dominion by grabbing at the forbidden fruit. Instead of gaining more dominion, they ended up shepherding the wind, or trying to. And we are left with that legacy. How can man "shepherd" the wind, rule it, control it, make it do his bidding? You cannot herd the wind like you can herd sheep or goats.

In other words, such power does not lie within man's reach. It will elude us. God alone is the true Shepherd (Eccl. 12:11).

Not only is attempting to gain leverage about as realistic as trying to be a shepherd to the breezes, but it leads to mental frustration. Solomon is a scholar and an intellectual. His wisdom, by God's gracious gift, surpasses that of anyone else. Yet Solomon finds that wisdom here is of no help to him. "For in much wisdom is much vexation, and he who increases knowledge increases sorrow" (1:18). This, too, takes us back to the story of Adam and Eve and the serpent. A variant on the Hebrew word "to know" is used three times in Ecclesiastes 3:17. That was the original temptation—by eating the fruit of the Tree of Knowledge, Adam and Eve would know the secrets of god-like power and wisdom. Solomon would agree with the German proverb "Much knowledge gives one a headache." Comprehensive knowledge, the kind of knowledge that would be the key to life's enigmas, always escapes man's intellectual grasp.

How should we respond to this? By turning to God and trusting him! John Calvin said it well.

> Each of us must, then, be so stung by the consciousness of our own unhappiness as to attain at least some knowledge of God. Thus, from the feeling of our own ignorance, vanity, poverty, infirmity, and—what is more—depravity and corruption, we recognize that the true light of wisdom, sound virtue, full abundance of every good, and purity of righteousness rest in the Lord alone. To this extent we are prompted by our own ills to contemplate the good things of God; and we cannot seriously aspire to him before we become displeased with ourselves . . . Accordingly, the knowledge of ourselves not only arouses us to seek God, but also, as it were, lead us by the hand to find him. (*Institutes of the Christian Religion* 1.1.1)

Our own ills should prompt us to look to God. Novelist Gene Wolfe has written a beautiful tetrology *The Book of the Long Sun*. In it his protagonist, Patera Silk, is drawn away from the pagan gods he serves by the true God. As he begins to understand the meaning of creation, he tells a young disciple: "A child who burns its hand says the fire's bad, as the saying goes; but the fire itself is saying,

'Not to me, child. Reach out to him.' " (*Epiphany of the Long Sun* [New York: Orb Books, 2000], 673). Nature and death are saying the same thing when they turn our labors into vapor. *Reach out to him.* Our frustration at trying to shepherd the wind should give us reason to turn to the one who rules the wind, the Spirit who is like the wind or "breath" (John 3:8). The one enthroned in the midst of smoke and cloud (Isa. 6:1–4; Eze. 1; Ex. 40; 1 Kings 8:10) can *alone* deal with the vaporous nature of life. Knowing this, we must entrust our lives to him.

SOLOMON'S TWO TESTS

Solomon moves on now to evaluate of two specific human endeavors under the sun. From verses one through eleven we have his investigation into man's search for joy. Then in verses twelve through sixteen we are led to contemplate the sort of wisdom that is viewed as a means of gain or leverage in the world. This is a long section (2:1–17) which deserves sustained attention.

> I said in my heart, "Come now, I will test you with pleasure; enjoy yourself." But behold, this also was vapor. I said of laughter, "It is mad," and of pleasure, "What use is it?" I searched with my heart how to cheer my body with wine—my heart still guiding me with wisdom—and how to lay hold on folly, till I might see what was good for the children of man to do under heaven during the few days of their life. I made great works. I built houses and planted vineyards for myself. I made myself gardens and parks, and planted in them all kinds of fruit trees. I made myself pools from which to water the forest of growing trees. I bought male and female slaves, and had slaves who were born in my house. I had also great possessions of herds and flocks, more than any who had been before me in Jerusalem. I also gathered for myself silver and gold and the treasure of kings and provinces. I got singers, both men and women, and many concubines, the delight of the children of man.
>
> So I became great and surpassed all who were before me in Jerusalem. Also my wisdom remained with me. And whatever my eyes desired I did not keep from them. I kept my heart from

> no pleasure, for my heart found pleasure in all my toil, and this was my reward for all my toil. Then I considered all that my hands had done and the toil I had expended in doing it, and behold, all was [vapor] and a striving after wind, and there was nothing to be gained under the sun.
>
> So I turned to consider wisdom and madness and folly. For what can the man do who comes after the king? Only what has already been done. Then I saw that there is more gain in wisdom than in folly, as there is more gain in light than in darkness. The wise person has his eyes in his head, but the fool walks in darkness. And yet I perceived that the same event happens to all of them. Then I said in my heart, "What happens to the fool will happen to me also. Why then have I been so very wise?" And I said in my heart that this also is [vapor]. For of the wise as of the fool there is no enduring remembrance, seeing that in the days to come all will have been long forgotten. How the wise dies just like the fool! So I hated life, because what is done under the sun was grievous to me, for all is [vapor] and [shepherding the wind].

In keeping with Calvin's observation that the knowledge of ourselves not only arouses us to seek God, but also, as it were, "leads us by the hand to find him," Solomon's quest for true wisdom ends with self-awareness. This knowledge of himself is specifically the futility of his attempts to wrestle joy and meaning from life by means of his own frantic endeavors under the sun.

When Solomon says in Ecclesiastes 2:9, "So I became great and surpassed all who were before me in Jerusalem," he is not referring to some great act of selfishness. God blessed him (initially, at least) with and for his people. We see this from elsewhere in the Bible:

> Judah and Israel were as many as the sand by the sea. They ate and drank and were happy. Solomon ruled over all the kingdoms from the Euphrates to the land of the Philistines and to the border of Egypt. They brought tribute and served Solomon all the days of his life. Solomon's provision for one day was thirty cors of fine flour and sixty cors of meal, ten fat oxen, and twenty pasture-fed cattle, a hundred sheep, besides deer, gazelles, roebucks, and fattened fowl. For he had dominion over all the region west of the Euphrates from Tiphsah to Gaza, over all the kings west of the

> Euphrates. And he had peace on all sides around him. And Judah and Israel lived in safety, from Dan even to Beersheba, every man under his vine and under his fig tree, all the days of Solomon. (1 Kings 4:20–25)

The description of the food Solomon provided is too much for one person or even one family to eat. It was for others. In 1 Kings 10:14 and following we have a further picture of Solomon's great wealth and the wealth he made available for many until silver was "as common in Jerusalem as stone" (1 Kings 10:9).

In the midst of this great blessing, Solomon makes a discovery: "But behold, this also was vapor. I said of laughter, 'It is mad,' and of pleasure, 'What use is it?' " (Eccl. 2:2). As Solomon was not being selfish, neither was he being self-indulgent. He is not saying, "When the books don't give the answer, then pass the bottle." He is clear that he was still guided by wisdom this whole time (2:3).

Solomon is seeking that which is *good*, that which will give him real power or an advantage in the world over his life and destiny. Notice the question in verse two regarding pleasure: "What use is it?" Or, as the NASB (New American Standard Bible) puts it, "What does it *accomplish*?" (emphasis added). The word translated as "pleasure" in the ESV could just as easily be interpreted as *mirth* or *joy*. What did this wise man find that joy gained for him? "Then I considered all that my hands had done and the toil I had expended in doing it, and behold, all was [vapor] and a striving after wind, and there was nothing to be gained under the sun" (2:11). Solomon highlights the fact that our advantage or ultimate profit or gain cannot be found on earth during one's lifetime ("under the sun"). Not even joy can accomplish anything that is not vaporous. The apostle Paul repeats this wisdom and applies it to the gospel: "If in this life only we have hoped in Christ, we are of all people most to be pitied" (1 Cor. 15:19).

Solomon confesses that, in some ways, wisdom is preferable to folly. "Then I saw that there is more gain in wisdom than in folly" (Eccl. 2:13). But this is a statement of faith, not of sight or experience. Ultimately one also finds the pursuit of wisdom is mere mist:

"I came to realize that the same fate awaits them both" (2:14). Death! As the book unfolds, Solomon comes face to face with death, man's universal and unavoidable end—the culmination of God's burdening man with "painful work." This shepherd king contemplates his own death (2:15) and asks himself the question: Why should I be wise? What advantage does the wise man or woman have, then? He answers it: "This too is [vapor]"—mysterious, impossible to grasp or understand. Remember, Solomon is not saying that wisdom is meaningless, but that the meaning eludes man. He exhorts us to follow his example and arrive at the same conclusion: "For what can the man do who comes after the king? Only what has already been done" (2:12).

This section of Ecclesiastes often gives evangelicals the heebie-jeebies. All this talk of pursuing pleasure and wine and riches—indeed, all the delights of the children of man—registers "worldliness" in many Christians' minds. Our first-glance interpretation might be that Solomon has lost his piety in the quest narrated here. Such a judgment fails to read the account carefully and look for the deeper meaning. It may be helpful for our understanding to consider Solomon's quest in the context of the corporate worship of his time.

As a boy, Solomon grew up immersed in the newly restructured corporate worship that his father David inspired through his composition of the psalms, his invention and orchestration of various musical instruments, and his use of the Levites as professional musicians, music directors, and choirs. David had composed the psalms some thirty years earlier, so they would have been quite familiar to the young prince Solomon. The content of the Psalter became the inspiration and source of Solomon's meditation on life and the world. Surely Psalm 45 forms the background for the Song of Solomon. In Psalm 49, for example, Solomon would have sung this:

> For he sees that even the wise die;
> the fool and the stupid alike must perish
> and leave their wealth to others. (v. 10)

And this:

> Be not afraid when a man becomes rich,
> when the glory of his house increases.
> For when he dies he will carry nothing away;
> his glory will not go down after him. (vv. 16–17)

Singing this before God in worship causes Solomon to reflect on how this applies to his own situation. Notice how these themes are amplified in Ecclesiastes—men die like beasts (Eccl. 3:19ff) and nothing man creates will endure (Eccl. 2:21ff). It's one thing to sing and hear these things, but Solomon was moved to *experience* them and intensified their impact on future generations of godly readers.

In our present section, for example, Solomon learns that work, houses, riches, influence, joy, even wisdom are all ephemeral, and worse, they cannot give a man any leverage or advantage in the end (2:11). He had heard this in the assembly when the congregation sang Psalm 73, but in God's plan Solomon would grow up and experience these things in order to deepen Israel's appreciation of God's Word and enable them to remain steadfast in their faith in the midst of many similar temptations. After Solomon's experience, he can second the psalmist's faith that God will bring prosperous wicked to judgment in the end. The psalmist learns this in the sanctuary of God (Ps. 73:17). Solomon, however, after hearing this in the gathered assembly of worshippers, must himself confirm this truth outside of the sanctuary in the world. Therefore, Solomon tells us there is nothing in all of this wealth and joy—no profit, no leverage, no lasting peace.

This is Solomon's extraordinary calling—to shoulder these burdens in order to educate his peers and guide future generations like us. Instead of hastily judging Solomon, as if he simply snapped and went on the equivalent of an ancient road trip with his drinking buddies, we should take Solomon's own repeated caveat seriously—all that he says he did here in 2:1–11 was done with his "heart still guiding him in wisdom" (2:3). He didn't become a fool temporarily to learn these things; rather, he assures us "my wisdom remained with me" (2:9). What this means is that when we read Ecclesiastes, we should give thanks that God put Solomon through the wringer so that we might partake in his wisdom. This is the purpose of wisdom literature, indeed of most books in general. They tell us what life is really like even before we have to experience it ourselves.

FALSE EXPECTATIONS

Music has become an industry and obsession in the modern and post-modern world. It is now economically and technologically possible for most people to afford the company of professional musicians. If one has a job that allows music to be played in the workplace, a person can virtually experience a soundtrack during every conscious moment of life. Summer vacations are like that for many teens.

Like all blessings, music can become a curse. Music is a wonderful gift, but our culture shows what can happen when it becomes an obsession and is treated as a god. Think of how a young man in college might feel if his mother told him she was going to sell the house and buy a van so that they could travel the country to follow a rock band on tour. He could easily come to hate the music after seeing how it was being treated. Much more, if someone were raised in a family that treated music or some style of music as if it were supposed to be the world's salvation (consider the way many idolized Wagnerian operas—beginning with Wagner himself—and the results of that idolatry in Germany), one would *have* to come to hate music in order simply to mature. He would have to hate music because music would be full of false promises to him. In fact, hating music would be a necessary step toward coming to the point where one could truly appreciate music for what it really is. While music is wonderful in its place, anyone who tries to gain real leverage with it will find that it is only vapor. This applies to all our anxious work, as Solomon makes clear in 2:18–23:

> I hated all my toil in which I toil under the sun, seeing that I must leave it to the man who will come after me, and who knows whether he will be wise or a fool? Yet he will be master of all for which I toiled and used my wisdom under the sun. This also is [vapor]. So I turned about and gave my heart up to despair over all the toil of my labors under the sun, because sometimes a person who has toiled with wisdom and knowledge and skill must leave everything to be enjoyed by someone who did not toil for it. This also is [vapor] and a great evil. What has a man from all the toil and striving of heart with which he toils beneath the sun? For all his days are full of sorrow, and his work is a vexation. Even in the night his heart does not rest. This also is [vapor].

Solomon is not being impious when he declares "I hated life" and "I hated all my toil in which I toil under the sun." Solomon is being *pious* to hate life. After all, loving life for the sake of the power of his toil would demonstrate that he lacked faith and was embracing idolatrous delusions rather than trusting God.

People develop idolatrous expectations of life by ignoring or discounting death. Death is an inescapable message from God, and it is not good news. While this seems obvious, it is resisted. Many commonly attempt to escape the real implications of death by claiming that one's work will be carried on or enjoyed by someone else, however, what happens after death is completely outside our control. "I must leave it to the man who will come after me, and who knows whether he will be wise or a fool?" (2:18, 19). Solomon rejects all false hope, all idolatry that would evade the vaporous nature of life when it comes to man's labor.

As we read the Bible, we often find ways to judge the piety of the biblical characters when in truth it is *their* piety that should judge the reader. Job is an example alongside Solomon. In Job 3 we see Job cursing the day of his birth. It is easy to see this as some sort of sin, forgetting that Job's temptation was to "curse God and die" (Job 2:9). Instead of cursing God, who has taken away everything and afflicted him, Job curses himself. This is an act of loyalty to God in the face of great temptation to be disloyal. Jeremiah's case is similar (Jer. 20:7–18). Likewise, Solomon hates life because he refuses to embrace lies that would comfort him in the face of death. He acknowledges God, even when God has afflicted man so that his labor brings him no advantage. His declaration that "I turned about and gave my heart up to despair over all the toil of my labors under the sun" (v. 20) uses language that expresses deepest feelings. Language like this is also found in Job and Jeremiah, the books of two suffering saints.

Solomon is appalled at life as a whole, the existence of man under the sun. He pours out deep feelings of revulsion at this situation. It is all *ra'* in Hebrew—grievous, disastrous, painful, afflicting, intolerable, distressing (2:21). It is *hebel*, as vapor enigmatic and elusive. Death robs man of any leverage or surplus in this life. Specifically, it takes away any advantage from his "toil," a key word in verses eighteen through twenty-three. God has ordained frustration for man's work. This frustration is epitomized in the discovery that everything you work for will be passed on to another—and you cannot control whether he will be a wise man or a fool. The problem is not so much that it will be passed on, but rather that "Who knows what kind of person he or she will be?" (2:19). There is nothing to guarantee the wisdom of your successors.

I know a Christian economist who is virtually obsessed with this problem, the question of inheritance and insuring that our children will pass on our inheritance to their children. It constantly happens that parents work and strive for things that their children devalue and lose. The ones who receive it all without working for it take their fortune for granted and squander it.

This should also provide us with a word of caution as well about what we are promised in books on Christian childrearing. We have the promise of God for them (Gen. 17:7), but so much of it depends upon how they respond to the grace of God in their lives. It is out of our control. There is no way to insure that your children will be faithful. What happened to all the glory given to David and Solomon? Their heirs gradually wasted it. Solomon himself was a "person who . . . toiled with wisdom and knowledge and skill [and] must leave everything to be enjoyed by someone who did not toil for it" (2:21). The future our toil and labor is *hebel*.

We appear here to have a defeated, despairing Solomon—a thoroughly pessimistic man. What does man accomplish? The wind cannot be herded and controlled. What advantage does our toil bring to us? In all of man's work and labor, he changes nothing, he controls nothing; everything goes on the same as it has, for everything is outside of his control! What is left? What is man to do? Are we to drown in our own self-pity? The question is asked again in verses twenty-two and twenty-three. "What does a man get?"

Solomon does not end this passage in despair. His conclusion (2:24–26), in fact, is quite upbeat.

> There is nothing better for a person than that he should eat and drink and find enjoyment in his toil. This also, I saw, is from the hand of God, for apart from him who can eat or who can have enjoyment? For to the one who pleases him God has given wisdom and knowledge and joy, but to the sinner he has given the business of gathering and collecting, only to give to one who pleases God. This also is [vapor] and [shepherding the wind].

At first glance this partial conclusion may not even seem consistent with his earlier laments unless we remember that Solomon has always been specific in his criticisms. He does not despair of life itself, but of "toil," of "work." Ultimately, this is *hebel* and a great disaster, for death is universal and no one can control the fruits of his labor once he is dead.

What if we regarded our labors and the temporary fruits we sometimes enjoy from them not as a means of power, but rather as gracious gifts? Solomon reminds the believer that a man's work is a gift from God (2:24). As long as he does not attempt to misuse work, to transform his God-given activities into a means of leveraging God and his creation for his own purposes, he can rejoice. All three goals that humans set for themselves—wisdom, knowledge, and joy—are gifts of God! God gives them to the one who pleases him—in a limited way, to be sure, but nevertheless in a real way. The wicked who cannot give up their quest for advantage will ultimately be frustrated in their attempt to seize these gifts of God. God will see to it at the end that everything that the wicked have accomplished is handed over to the righteous (2:26).

In spite of life's vaporous nature, God can be trusted. God and life can be enjoyed despite the fact that life cannot be mastered, leveraged, or even fully comprehended by man. Solomon uses the word *hebel* as a description of the enigmatic, mysterious, intractable character of life under the sun for man—even for the Christian man! Faith recognizes this and, in the face of it, moves forward to claim and enjoy the life and work and happiness that God apportions as gifts to man.

Realizing this can help you deal with life in a way that honors God. For example, do not be surprised to find yourself in a frustrating situation from which you cannot escape by means of controlling it. Not everything can be fixed! Not everything is a problem to be solved. Some things must be borne, must be suffered and endured. Wisdom does not teach us how to master the world. It does not give us techniques for programming life such that life becomes orderly and predictable.

In fact, trying to gain a wisdom that will give you control may make you worse off. It is precisely the *task*, the *work*, the *endeavor*, the *toil* of mastering life that is vapor—a chasing after dust devils! Instead of gaining leverage, you will only add to your frustration. Solomon carries out a direct frontal assault on the very idea that humanity is able to leverage creation for his own purposes, to wrestle order out of God's inscrutable ways. Wisdom—real biblical wisdom—is not the art of steering or programming the world according to man's purposes. Wisdom does not advise man to search for *order* or to attempt to *master* life. Under the sun, one cannot know, one cannot predict, one cannot trace causal connections. Who knows why things happen? Often, trying to figure it out is simply chasing after the wind as if we can catch and contain it. One can only hope and believe. Rejoice in what God has given you to do and trust in him. This the perspective of faith.

If control is ultimately not an option, what should you strive for? "There is nothing better for a person than that he should eat and drink and find enjoyment in his toil" (Eccl. 1:24). Make it your ambition to lead a quiet life, rejoicing in God's good gifts to you. "Better is a handful of quietness than two hands full of toil and [shepherding the wind]" (Eccl. 4:6). Christian wisdom advocates celebration, rejoicing, and enjoying what God has given for you to enjoy. Solomon's advice is for you to cherish the small gifts that come your way from God. Man's true lot in this world is not primarily understood in terms of hard work, but in joyous reception of the gifts of God. Approach life receptively; enjoy God's gifts as they unfold.

We Christians who have the privilege of the New Testament Scriptures ought to accept the wisdom of Solomon because his advice is found repeatedly in the letters of the apostle Paul. In the New Testament it remains true that a handful of quietness is preferable to two hands full of toil and shepherding the wind.

> Aspire to live quietly, and to mind your own affairs, and to work with your hands, as we instructed you. (1 Thess. 4:11)

> Pray for kings and all who are in high positions, that we may lead a peaceful and quiet life, godly and dignified in every way. (1 Tim. 2:2)

> For we hear that some among you walk in idleness, not busy at work, but busybodies. Now such persons we command and encourage in the Lord Jesus Christ to do their work quietly and to earn their own living. (2 Thess. 3:11–12)

> Each one should remain in the condition in which he was called. Were you a slave when called? Do not be concerned about it. But if you can gain your freedom, avail yourself of the opportunity. For he who was called in the Lord as a slave is a freedman of the Lord. Likewise he who was free when called is a slave of Christ. You were bought with a price; do not become slaves of men. So, brothers, in whatever condition each was called, there let him remain with God. (1 Cor. 7:20–24)

Finally, Ecclesiastes should remind us to accept the posture ingrained into us by the public worship of God in thanksgiving with the people of God.

My role in life is not primarily that of an author but of a preacher and a pastor. In our Sunday morning service for the congregation in which I serve, the Lord's Supper is a part of our regular weekly worship. As I preached through this part of Ecclesiastes, I was able to tell my congregation that our own actions in worship reflected the attitude of faith promoted by Solomon. At the Table which the Lord spreads for us, our minds and hearts are trained in how to relate to all of life. All is a gift. All of life is represented in the bread and wine—all of material creation. We receive it and give thanks for it. There is every reason to think that Solomon is referring to the ritual covenant meals that the Israelites enjoy in fellowship with God when he writes, "[n]othing is better for a man than that he should eat and drink, and that his soul should enjoy good in his labor. This also, I saw, was from the hand of God." (Eccl. 2:24). Compare this to the descriptions of the old covenant feasts, such as this one:

> You shall tithe all the yield of your seed that comes from the field year by year. And before the LORD your God, in the place that he will choose, to make his name dwell there, you shall eat the tithe of your grain, of your wine, and of your oil, and the firstborn of your herd and flock, that you may learn to fear the LORD your God always. And if the way is too long for you, so that you are not able to carry the tithe, when the LORD your God blesses you, because the place is too far from you, which the LORD your God chooses, to set his name there, then you shall turn it into money and bind up the money in your hand and go to the place that the LORD your God chooses and spend the money for whatever you desire—oxen or sheep or wine or strong drink, whatever your appetite craves. And you shall eat there before the LORD your God and rejoice, you and your household. (Deut. 14:22–26)

Human life in all its mystery is a gift from God. The man of God will experience frustration and pain, and he will respond with deep feelings of revulsion and even hatred; this must only be a temporary posture, a passing response. The ultimate posture of the wise believer is to "take and eat," confessing that God has gifted him with life.

Part Two

Ecclesiastes 3:1–5:20

We need to stop and remember where we are in Solomon's work. He has finished the first of four sections in his book (chapters 1 and 2). He will now elaborate on his themes, clarifying and intensifying them, from verse one of chapter 3 until he reaches his second provisional conclusion in Ecclesiastes 5:18–20. He develops his case in three steps (3:1–5:17):

3:1–15	Solomon begins with a confession of faith. God is lord of the times. He has a plan that embraces every man, woman, and child, and all their actions. His plan is fitting and good.
3:16–4:16	Solomon next examines troubling anomalies and apparent contradictions to the confession of God's all-encompassing plan.
5:1–17	Finally, Solomon cautions the believer on how to live with this confession and in the light of these anomalies.

In this way he reaches his second partial conclusion:

> Behold, what I have seen to be good and fitting is to eat and drink and find enjoyment in all the toil with which one toils under the sun the few days of his life that God has given him, for this is his lot. Everyone also to whom God has given wealth and possessions and power to enjoy them, and to accept his lot and rejoice in his toil—this is the gift of God. For he will not much remember the days of his life because God keeps him occupied with joy in his heart. (5:18–20)

Notice that this is not merely a restatement of the conclusion to his first inquiry (2:24–26), but includes dimensions appropriate to his musings in this new section. The basics are still there—the admonition to eat and drink, to find satisfaction in one's labor, and to enjoy what God has given you. But now we have a few other things. We are assured that this life is "fitting" or "proper" in verse eighteen. Furthermore, it is fitting because "this is his lot" or heritage or portion. This language, reminiscent of God's giving the land to Israel and apportioning a lot to each tribe and family for their heritage, is repeated twice. The wise man will gratefully "accept his lot." You and I have been given a heritage from God in our work and in whatever else we have. That is God's gift along with all the trials and frustrations. Living by faith means enjoying all that God has given us for what it truly is: his gift. This is fitting and proper.

Finally, we are given an additional *purpose* for this other than sheer enjoyment: "For he will not much remember the days of his life because God keeps him occupied with joy in his heart." The answer to an unhealthy preoccupation with finding the answers and reasons for all of one's troubles is to enjoy what you have to enjoy, including your toil, without trying to figure out some sort of ultimate leverage or advantage from it.

We arrive at the same conclusion as before, but in a way that is now deepened and developed to include a confession on the part of the believer. This confession means that he will accept life as a gift from God and accept his limited place without fretting over an attempt to pry into God's secret purposes which remain hidden from him.

5

THE BURDEN OF ETERNITY IN OUR HEARTS: ECCLESIASTES 3:1–15

And which of you by being anxious can add a single hour to his span of life? —Matthew 6:27

Back in the early nineties when Steven Covey was just making the big time with his "seven habits" and everyone who was anyone sported a leather-bound notebook planner, a young upwardly-mobile man named Jim found himself sitting next to a pretty brunette on a business flight. Trying to figure out how to strike up a conversation, he complimented her on her thick, multi-tabbed scheduler.

"Oh, yes," she said, warming immediately to the subject, "I love this thing. My life would be chaos without it."

"I use a small one for appointments," said Jim. "but I'm still a novice. Have you managed to get in the habit of doing all that goal-setting? Is it helpful?"

His new acquaintance was already nodding vigorously before Jim finished his questions. "Oh yes, I try to think ahead about how much time I have to afford on things I have to do."

They exchanged chitchat. Jim found out that her name was Lily and that her maternal grandparents lived in the same area as his sister. Since she obviously liked to talk about her planner, he returned to that subject. "How far ahead do you plan?"

"It depends," she replied. "Sometimes years."

"Years?" he repeated incredulously.

"Actually, it's hard to tell. I've got some stuff scheduled for my mother's death. She's alive right now and her health is pretty good, so I assume that it is probably years away."

"You've already made funeral arrangements and all that?"

"Oh, I didn't mean that sort of thing," said Lily. "I'll worry about that later. What I've prepared for is the grieving."

"Grieving?"

"Sure. I have a pretty busy job. I figure that I can work in the grieving process by scheduling it for an hour each night for three weeks. That way, if I have the funeral on a weekend, I won't need to miss any work."

"You think you can plan when you are sad about your mother's death?"

"Well, of course!" exclaimed Lily, sounding surprised Jim would even ask. "What's the point of having this," she asked as she patted her planner, "if you don't use it to schedule your time?"

Obviously, this is a fictional story. People do not usually claim to be able to decide when they will weep and when they rejoice. The fact that there is a time and season for everything doesn't mean we have any power over when these times and seasons occur.

We all experience it. You knew you had to leave on time, but getting the children into the car, having to deal with an unexpected desperate search for the keys, and hearing the phone ring just as you were heading out the door, all conspired to make you late. Frustration made you snap at those around you, and you became so distracted that you made more mistakes, which delayed you further. The Lord has set the times of our lives and we must confess his sovereignty without anxiety. Listen to Solomon's poetic description of this truth.

> For everything there is a season, and a time for every matter under heaven:
> a time to be born, and a time to die;
> a time to plant, and a time to pluck up what is planted;
> a time to kill, and a time to heal;
> a time to break down, and a time to build up;
> a time to weep, and a time to laugh;
> a time to mourn, and a time to dance;
> a time to cast away stones, and a time to gather stones together;
> a time to embrace, and a time to refrain from embracing;
> a time to seek, and a time to lose;
> a time to keep, and a time to cast away;
> a time to tear, and a time to sew;
> a time to keep silence, and a time to speak;
> a time to love, and a time to hate;
> a time for war, and a time for peace. (Eccl. 3:1–8)

The Rolling Stones were wrong. Time is not on our side. We don't control it. We can't stop it or speed it up. That is Solomon's point in this passage. He is not writing lyrics for The Byrds' hit song "Turn, Turn, Turn." This is not an advertisement for an office management philosophy. Whatever habits highly effective people might have or acquire, they do not have control over time. The sixteenth-century reformer Martin Luther understood this passage when he explained it this way:

> You should understand this [Eccl. 3:1–8] as follows: All human works and efforts have a certain and definite time of acting, of beginning, and of ending, *beyond human control*. Thus this is spoken in opposition to free will. It is not up to us to prescribe the time, the manner, or the effect of the things that are to be done; and so it is obvious that here our strivings and efforts are unreliable. Everything comes and goes at the time that God has appointed. He proves this on the basis of examples of *human works*

> *whose times lie outside the choice of man.* From this he draws the conclusion that it is useless for men to be tormented by their strivings and that they do not accomplish anything, even though they were to burst, unless the proper time and the hour appointed by God has come. . . . So the power of God comprehends all things in definite hours, so that they cannot be hindered by anyone. (*Luther's Works* 15 [Concordia Publishing House], 49)

This is as good an interpretation of this passage in Ecclesiastes as I have ever read. To understand Solomon's wisdom, it might be good to consider the antithesis of Spiritual wisdom in a notorious statement of worldly wisdom. Compare it with W. E. Henley's infamous poem *Invictus*:

> In the fell clutch of circumstance
> I have not winced nor cried aloud.
> Under the bludgeons of chance
> My head is bloody, but unbowed.
>
> It matters not how strait the gate,
> How charged with punishments the scroll,
> I am the master of my fate;
> I am the captain of my soul.

This is autonomous man's song, the gauntlet he throws down to the sovereign God. Such a man insists either that he is able to control the times or else that he is at least able to resist their effect on his life deep in his soul. The seasons may have bloodied him, but they did not make him bow.

Against such arrogance, Solomon now offers us godly wisdom. Solomon's thesis is that behind all of man's activity is the all-encompassing plan of God. Every action of man, every event that comes upon man, can be traced to the all-embracing determination of God as its ultimate source.

From the start we get a hint that the issue is not primarily human activity or our determination to find the opportune time to act a certain way. "For everything there is a season, and a time for every matter under heaven" (Eccl. 3:1). The noun "season" is the

Hebrew word that means "appointed time" or "predetermined season." It is too often sentimentalized and romanticized—taken out of its proper context in Solomon's overall argument. So the poem is often read to mean that there are appropriate moments for people to act and at the proper moment even ordinarily objectionable behavior can be "beautiful in its own way."

Unfortunately, this is not what the poem is about. It is not about human determination of events or even human discernment of times and seasons. The poetic passage is about God's activity, not man's. It is about God's comprehensive determination of all of man's times (contextually see 3:11, 17 for more evidence of this). Indeed, it sets the stage for the focus in this entire second section (3:1–5:20) which is about the activity of God, the all-encompassing plan of God, and the appropriate human response to whatever God does.

Be careful not to "spiritualize" this list as some have attempted to do. There's no need to attempt to interpret these actions as signifying "spiritual things." Some commentators, looking for "religious" meaning in this passage, think that Solomon meant to signify spiritual regeneration by "birth" and the death of the sin nature by "a time to die." Or "a time to plant" means a time to instill truth in the heart and by "uprooting" Solomon means the rooting out of sin in the heart of man. And a time to kill refers to the mortification of sin and a time to heal, the spiritual healing of holiness, and so on.

This is a travesty. It robs these words of their real force. Solomon is referring to normal life. God's plan—his timing—extends to birth and death, sickness and health, employment and unemployment. The entirety of human life is poetically summed up here.

Notice that God's plan includes even those situations that appear to be in the hands of men. Thus we read in verse three of a time to kill and a time to heal, a time to tear down and a time to build. While humans pretend to control such decisions, they are not the ones in control. They are no more in control of such things than they are of their emotional responses. According to verse four, God appoints even our emotions. There is "a time to weep, and a time to laugh." We cannot control such times. You cannot plan how long or short a time you will spend grieving over the death of a loved one. You don't even determine when your loved ones will die. God decides that.

Think about how much our decisions are dependent on factors that we know we have no control over. At one time a stone is useless and cast away; at another time it is useful and gathered up (3:5a). At one point in history oil is simply a curiosity; at another point it is a precious resource and the most important factor in our standard of living. In the same way we embrace many people and things at one time that we later refrain from embracing (3:5b). We respond to the situations God puts us in. These things are forced upon us by factors outside our control. It is in God's hands.

God's providence even extends to the calamites of life such as hate and war (3:8). Here Solomon is following the clear message of Scripture. We read in Psalm 105:25, "He turned their hearts to hate his people, to deal craftily with his servants." Moses says the same thing in Exodus 11:3, "And the Lord gave the people favor in the sight of the Egyptians. Moreover, the man Moses was very great in the land of Egypt, in the sight of Pharaoh's servants and in the sight of the people." All these things are under God's control.

Are you constantly frustrated that you are not accomplishing enough? Are you unable to be satisfied because you lack control over your life? Do you constantly try to read more to gain insight that will gain an advantage? Ecclesiastes is asking you to reconsider your stance toward life. Controlling the times and seasons, or even understanding why God sends them when he does, is too great and marvelous a thing for anyone but God. There are other passages that especially speak to this sort of situation. Consider Psalm 131.

> O LORD, my heart is not lifted up;
>   my eyes are not raised too high;
> I do not occupy myself with things
>   too great and too marvelous for me.
> But I have calmed and quieted my soul,

like a weaned child with its mother;
like a weaned child is my soul within me.

O Israel, hope in the LORD
from this time forth and forevermore.

If we hope in the Lord, let us not pretend that there is something in our striving or our wisdom that is going to deliver us. Let us not lift up our hearts or our eyes. Solomon's observation calls for humble wisdom.

The list of "times" in Ecclesiastes 3:2–8 is not exhaustive, but it is representative of "everything" or "every matter" or season. Many commentators have tried to find a rationale for the order in Solomon's list, but there isn't one. Solomon is making a point by listing these fourteen pairs of opposing activities in no discernible order. That is the way the world is. That is the way our lives are. We cannot predict. We cannot determine. We cannot recognize a pattern. It sounds like noise rather than a signal. We find ourselves enmeshed in these seasons, but we have no sovereign determination over them. They come upon us. We are not in control. We have no *leverage*, no *advantage* over these seasons. Wisdom accepts these seasons from God's hand, and then follows God's lead by discerning the appropriate "dance step." Faithful and wise living means submitting to God's timetable and thereby responding in a way that acknowledges God's superior but inscrutable plan for your life.

ETERNITY IN OUR HEARTS

When you decide to go on a summer vacation with the family that involves many hours of interstate traveling, like everyone else, you use your atlas or web map engines to calculate how many hours it will take to arrive at your destination. Typically, if you have a number of children, especially younger ones, you instinctively add time to figure out how long the trip will take.

Nevertheless, despite your care and calculations, almost invariably your plans are highly inaccurate. Perhaps there are construction crews doing massive repairs on most or all of the interstates on your route, or you forget that you are trying to get through or around a major city during rush hour. Add to those possibilities the way an automobile accident can stop traffic and it becomes extremely likely that you will end up stuck in traffic, not going anywhere according to any timetable.

Have you ever found yourself in such circumstances—stuck on an interstate highway, stopped dead in a line of cars and trucks with no way out? What do you do? You get out of your car and try to get a glimpse ahead. You stand on your hood and look up and back, but all you see is an endless line of cars. If only you could see the end, or even the beginning! In a way, if you could simply forget that there was a destination for you, you would probably be able to deal better with the wait.

According to Solomon, God has caught us in this sort of frustrating trap. He has put eternity in our hearts, but we cannot see from God's eternal perspective the reason he has for assigning the times and seasons that he gives.

> What gain has the worker from his toil? I have seen the business that God has given to the children of man to be busy with. He has made everything fitting in its time. Also, he has put eternity into man's heart, yet so that he cannot find out what God has done from the beginning to the end. I know that there is nothing better for them than to be joyful and to do good as long as they live; also that everyone should eat and drink and take pleasure in all his toil—this is God's gift to man.
>
> I know that whatever God does endures forever; nothing can be added to it, nor anything taken from it. God has done it, so that people fear before him. That which is, already has been; that which is to be, already has been; and God seeks what has been driven away. (Eccl. 3:9–15)

To understand how this passage works, remember that Solomon has just given us a poem about the times of life (3:1–8). This leads him to ask again the question he asked at the beginning: "What gain has the worker from his toil?"

The answer is that all of the labor of man cannot alter the plan of God. We can never ensure only times of birth or times of planting, healing or laughing or dancing or gathering or love or peace. It all comes from God and he gives us both death and birth, killing and healing, plucking and planting, and much more besides. Because everything has its time from God, man cannot ultimately control God's providential administration of all events. No leverage can be gained and no advantage achieved.

Since Solomon is asking the same question he asked at the beginning of Ecclesiastes, you would expect the same sort of answer as before. Indeed, in verse ten Solomon seems merely to repeat himself: "I have seen the business that God has given to the children of man to be busy with." God has given each of us tasks or work—a preoccupation. If God controls the times, how can it be otherwise? Whether we are engaged in weddings or funerals or most other things in life will depend on what situations God bestows upon us. Our circumstances dictate what we must do and our circumstances are not under our control. Think of the plans we may have made before gas prices suddenly escalated. Suddenly everyone had to shift priorities and resources and either give up some travel or give up something else they used to be able to afford. Every time our lack of control over life is brought to our attention we tend to treat it as some sort of anomaly, but the fact is that all of life is like that.

Solomon is not merely repeating himself. He adds a statement that gives us a different light on what he has said. At the beginning of verse eleven the ESV puts it this way: God "has made everything beautiful in its time." Solomon is making a *confession of faith*.

Notice that in making this confession of faith, Solomon turns away *from* man's toil and questions of whether it gives leverage or advantage, and turns *to* God's action. God is the primary actor here. God is the principle doer or worker. While the idea is barely discernible at this point in the passage, Solomon quickly reinforces it in the same verse by speaking of "what God has done from the beginning to the end." And again in verse fourteen we read that "whatever God does endures forever; nothing can be added to it, nor anything taken from it. God has done it, so that people fear before him." God's labor is not vapor. Or to put it another way: God is able to shepherd the wind. He is not only *able* to do so, but he has told us that he *does* control all of what to us is unruly mist.

Notice also that no matter how senseless and out of control our lives seem to be, we are promised that God has made everything *fitting* for its time. The ESV's choice to translate the word as "beautiful" is maybe not the best option, given the immediate context. Solomon is not primarily making an aesthetic evaluation of God's work. The point is that God does indeed have a plan and that everything he has done is in keeping with that plan.

That means *everything*, birth and death, war and peace. No matter what it is, somehow it fits into God's plan. In human endeavors we can make foolish decisions because we don't see the point of a plan. It happens often on Christmas morning. Fathers and mothers diligently try to assemble their children's new toys, wading through multi-page instruction manuals. Often, a specific direction seems like nothing more than a waste of time. I remember when I assembled a swing set in the backyard and had to deal with pages and pages of instructions. Early on I was given directions to do something painstaking and completely senseless. Being wiser than my instruction booklet, I chose to bypass it and move on. Bad idea. After much effort, when the project should have been completed, it suddenly became clear that I had neglected an essential step in the plan. I had to go back and do everything all over again.

What was my problem? My problem was that I was not as wise as I thought I was. I didn't understand the whole plan, so that particular step did not look "fitting" to me. It did not appear suitable. I lacked the perspective of those who wrote the instruction manual. If you could see from God's perspective and know his plan as he does, then you would see that all the times that he ordains are suitable. They fit in their place, but you cannot see from God's perspective because you are not God.

LIVING BY FAITH

Through both teaching and example, Solomon is telling us that we must live by faith. We see this because Solomon's statement itself is nothing less than a confession of faith. Solomon has no argument for this confidence from observable data. He cannot prove from what he sees that God "has made everything suitable in its time." What he is articulating is a Christian confession, even though it is not within his comprehension. God's administration of the world is always and everywhere fitting and suitable, even though we can't see how. We are never able to understand, in this life, what all the different steps in the instruction manual are supposed to do. We can't see how the times that God gives us are fitting.

God's plan is like those pictures that you can't understand until you stand back, adjust your eyes and see the whole thing. Only in this case, you can never stand back far enough to make the picture come into focus. You cannot stand outside or above time as God does. Nevertheless, God's comprehensive work *is* fitting. Everything fits in. No matter what it is—whether birthing, dying, planting, uprooting, killing, healing, weeping, laughing, mourning, dancing, loving, hating, war, and peace—all of it is integrated in God's plan, which lies beyond man's ability to fathom.

Solomon goes on to say in the rest of verse eleven that "also, he has put eternity into man's heart, yet so that he cannot find out what God has done from the beginning to the end." There have been some different ideas among translators about what exactly, according to Solomon, God has put into our hearts, but "eternity" seems right. We have here an ironic statement. God has put in us a consciousness of—a yearning for—what transcends the present moment. We instinctively want to know "the beginning to the end." In a real way, if we could simply forget that there is a plan, we would probably be able to better deal with life, but God doesn't let us forget. We are stuck on the interstate and we know it. We are stuck without being able to see where we are going or it if is near or far. We are stuck between time and eternity.

Despite the irony of eternity in our hearts and the frustration it causes, Solomon is clear that it counts as a gift of God. Just as God has given men business to be busy with (3:10), so he has given men and women eternity in their hearts.

In light of this basic fact, Solomon expresses two personal certainties in the verses that follow. In both cases these certainties are marked out by his declaration "I know" in the beginning of verses twelve and fourteen, not "I perceived" as the ESV has it. The first of these certainties concerns what human beings ought to do and the second what God does and will do. Eternity in our hearts is supposed to reinforce to us that we are not the ones with the plan, but that God has the plan and we can trust him.

First, then, what is man to do? "I know that there is nothing better for them than to be joyful and to do good as long as they live; also that everyone should eat and drink and take pleasure in all his toil—this is God's gift to man" (3:12, 13). Men and women need to learn to accept the good gifts that God gives to them. We need to know that everything we are and possess is the gift of God. We need to learn to find satisfaction in the work that God has given us—to eat and drink with thankful hearts. Brooding, sulking, or cursing any aspect of God's particular work is out of place. The believer should enjoy what he has been given. There are many good and joyful reasons to build sandcastles, the tide notwithstanding.

In other words, we must live fully in the present. We can all learn a lesson from the title of the newsletter "Right Now Counts Forever" by Christian teacher, scholar, and leader R. C. Sproul. What I do right now, how I receive God's gifts, and how I find satisfaction in the times God has given me are the most important things in life. Life will be unbearable, a bewildering confusion of this and that, an impossible burden unless we confess what we have is a gift of God, whether we comprehend it or not. If we are wise, we will abandon all hope of comprehension and rest in God's good gifts to us. We will give up the illusion of gaining leverage with our toil, and enjoy it as God's grace.

Second, we must consider both what God does and will do: "I know that whatever God does endures forever; nothing can be added to it, nor anything taken from it. God has done it, so that people fear before him. That which is, already has been; that which is to be, already has been; and God seeks what has been driven away" (3:14, 15). Solomon's point here is not that God's actions will last forever. God's actions are beyond us; they are eternal.

In contrast, man is bound to the present. Man is unable to discover the activity of God from beginning to end. According to verse twelve we can "be happy" and do good "while we live," but God transcends this creaturely work. The past and present are open before God and are subject to his sovereign disposition. The times are what he determines as we saw in the last section dealing with 3:1–8. Nothing escapes the dominion of God. His works are eternal, and human activity cannot "add to or subtract from" the work of God!

What God wants to do will invariably be done; and no human being, no matter what efforts he makes, can alter the course of his life or the times and seasons God gives to us. We have no leverage over God. Solomon learned this confession of faith, and its basic importance, from the psalms—the songs of Israel's worship: "My times are in your hand; rescue me from the hand of my enemies and from my persecutors!" (Psa. 31:15).

Why does God then burden man with such a life? Why does he order the world just so? So that men will fear him (Eccl. 3:14). The "fear of God" appears in Ecclesiastes at crucial points (5:7; 7:18; 8:12–13; 12:13). Rather than searching for advantage, men and women should fear God. Fearing God is equivalent to trusting him. God wants us to trust him for all things and trust in him alone as he has revealed himself.

This is the beginning of all wisdom and godliness. It is the first command of the Ten Commandments. "And God spoke all these words, saying, I am the Yahweh your God, who brought you out of the land of Egypt, out of the house of slavery. You shall have no other gods before me." Yahweh is Lord. He does what he does, and his ways are to be feared and trusted rather than questioned.

These statements about the limitations on creaturely knowledge are deeply related to our need and duty to embrace the true God and reject idols. Human knowledge will eventually only take you so far. Solomon is a wise man. He knows our limitations. God is God and you are his creature. The question with which Solomon challenges you is this: Who is your *Lord*? Luther's comments on the first commandment are telling. He writes in his Large Catechism:

> A "god" means that from which we are to expect all good and to which we are to take refuge in all distress, so that to have a God is nothing else than to trust and believe Him from the [whole] heart; as I have often said that the confidence and faith of the heart alone make both God and an idol. If your faith and trust be right, then is your god also true; and, on the other hand, if your trust be false and wrong, then you have not the true God; for these two belong together faith and God. That now, I say, upon which you set your heart and put your trust is properly your god.

All things come from God. Thus we read in Romans 9:16, "So then it is not of him who wills or runs, but of God who shows mercy." God has shut man out of the control room of the world. Man must trust his Maker and Redeemer.

This trust and enjoyment of God's gifts will entail real worship. This is what is meant in verse fourteen when it says that "God has done it, so that people fear *before* him" (emphasis added). Solomon is not just referring to godly, wise attitudes that we should adopt, but also to something we do "before" God, that is, in his presence. The one who fears God dreads nothing more than God's disfavor. He will be driven to worship, to fear before the Lord by his own creaturely ignorance and inability to control the times of his life, and by the eternity in his heart with which the Lord has gifted him.

Thus, Solomon ends this section affirming God's sufficiency: "That which is, already has been; that which is to be, already has been; and God seeks what has been pursued." This refers us back to how Ecclesiastes began. While all man's toil is vapor, a futile attempt to shepherd the wind, God can do what man cannot do. He can actually catch and control the wind as well as the mists of life. He can bring about something good from all of man's toil, but we need to forget about accomplishing or comprehending that good ourselves. We must realize that there is no poetic justice in this life. God will judge in his good time.

Let the past be. God will take care of it. God's seeking out the past will result either in judgment (as we shall see in verse seventeen) or the restoration of the past and what has been lost. In either case, you and I are powerless and ought to leave these matters to God. From a human point of view things are lost—time is lost, people are lost, opportunity is lost, jobs are lost, wives are lost, husbands are lost—all of these things are chased away and lost in the past, unrecoverable for us.

At the last judgment God will "call back" the past. He will seek it out and connect it with the future. Nothing will be lost.

Solomon's message is *good news* for us. First, his wisdom in verses fourteen and fifteen releases us from the overwhelming responsibility of attempting godhood. The knowledge of God's comprehensive sovereign control should be a release. The burden of being a god is not one that a human creature was meant to shoulder. Along with godlike sovereignty comes the crushing responsibility for your entire life and the outcome of your life. Ecclesiastes is liberating. It tells you that you need not feel guilty for something you cannot control. All times and seasons are in God's hands.

To deny our creaturely dependence is really a denial of reality—the reality established for us by God. Such a denial is inherently enslaving even though it is presented as the key to freedom. This was true in the Garden of Eden and it is true now whenever people suppress the truth. For example, human-potential psychologists are fond of telling us that "we make our own reality." In conforming to their doctrine, the self becomes a god. Each individual must bear the weight of being a god to himself and others. He must create his own world. The self is supremely autonomous and supremely capable. We can never relax. Our own self-actualization demands our constant vigilance. Everything depends on us. We must control it all! As M. Scott Peck wrote in *The Road Less Traveled*, "As soon as we believe that it is possible for a man to become God, we can really never rest for long, never say, okay, my job is done. We must constantly push ourselves to greater and greater wisdom, greater and greater effectiveness. By this belief we will have trapped ourselves, at least until death, on an effortful treadmill of self-improvement and spiritual growth. God's responsibility must be our own."

Likewise, William Kirk Kilpatrick has observed that "the point is, when you have nothing and no one to rely on but yourself, life becomes very serious indeed. If in addition the self is made out by all the experts to be some sort of holy wonder machine, and if you have not yet found the switch, your burden is that much more." This is the treadmill of self-actualization and self-improvement. The self is God. The message of Ecclesiastes allows us to lay this burden down.

This leads to the next point. By fearing God we are enabled to be satisfied with our place in life and indeed rejoice in what God graciously gives us (3:12–13). Verses fourteen and fifteen confess God's faithfulness and so serve to ground the believer's fear of God. This fear of God is the fear the son has for a father; it is a positive, healthy, honoring fear of the one who is creator and controller of all of creation. It is the awe of faith.

Understanding the priority of faith allows us to consider the fullness of the faith that we have because of what God has done in Christ long after Solomon lived. We have a privileged position in the new covenant times and thus have, of course, an advantage over Solomon. We have better insight into God's plan. God's plan has been embodied, literally, in the person of his son. The darker side of life now makes more sense to us after the cross of Christ!

Recognize the real advance that has been made for us in the new covenant. Not only has God laid upon men a burden, as Solomon tells us, but also God has allowed himself to be laid upon as the gospel reveals to us. The burden that he laid upon men he has taken upon himself. Christ is the first and the last, the alpha and omega, the beginning and the end. In Christ, God makes our times and seasons his times and seasons.

6

Death and Friendship: Ecclesiastes 3:16–4:16

And let us consider how to stir up one another
to love and good works, not neglecting to meet together,
as is the habit of some, but encouraging one another, and
all the more as you see the Day drawing near. —*Hebrews 10:25*

A hymn we sometimes sing in my congregation, as in many other churches, is "Through all the changing scenes of life" by Nicholas Brady and Nathan Tate. Here is the fifth verse:

> O make but trial of his love;
>   experience will decide
> How blest they are, and only they,
>   who in his truth confide.

This hymn is largely but loosely based on Psalm 34. In paraphrasing psalms one always runs the risk of including something that is not the best, and I think this is one of those times. Even though I use the song in my congregation, I wince every time I sing that stanza. Be honest. Do you think it is perfectly fine to tell people that they can let *experience* decide whether or not God loves them? Doesn't Romans 1:18 tell us that it is God's wrath that is revealed from heaven, under the sun, rather than God's love?

I think Solomon would dispute this verse of the hymn as well. As a claim of faith the rest of the hymn works well, but experience in this life is *not* going to do what this hymn claims. Experience is precisely that which will not make known to you the love of God. Experience can never ultimately decide. Solomon would say that we normally experience life first as curse—a judgment—not blessing. Once again, hear the shepherd king's wise words:

> Moreover, I saw under the sun that in the place of justice, even there was wickedness, and in the place of righteousness, even there was wickedness. I said in my heart, God will judge the righteous and the wicked, for there is a time for every matter and for every work. I said in my heart with regard to the children of man that God is testing them that they may see that they themselves are but beasts. For what happens to the children of man and what happens to the beasts is the same; as one dies, so dies the other. They all have the same breath, and man has no advantage over the beasts, for all is [vapor]. All go to one place. All are from the dust, and to dust all return. Who knows whether the spirit of man goes upward and the spirit of the beast goes down into the earth? So I saw that there is nothing better than that a man should rejoice in his work, for that is his lot. Who can bring him to see what will be after him? (Eccl. 3:16–22)

We experience life under the sun as "the burden, the work of affliction that God has laid upon the Sons of Adam" (Eccl. 1:13). Adam and Eve before the fall would have experienced life and the world first as *blessing*, but all of their posterity experiences the world and life first as a *curse*. Everyone who is honest with himself will admit to being frustrated by wave after wave of experiences in life that apparently contradict our confession of God's goodness and all-encompassing plan. We can try to sugarcoat our situation with a great deal of "pious" talk, and in many churches believers feel pressured to do so, but it simply isn't true. The Bible itself tells us this. Consider Psalm 73:1–12:

> Truly God is good to Israel,
>   to those who are pure in heart.
> But as for me, my feet had almost stumbled,
>   my steps had nearly slipped.
> For I was envious of the arrogant
>   when I saw the prosperity of the wicked.
> For they have no pangs until death;
>   their bodies are fat and sleek.
> They are not in trouble as others are;
>   they are not stricken like the rest of mankind.
> Therefore pride is their necklace;
>   violence covers them as a garment.
> Their eyes swell out through fatness;
>   their hearts overflow with follies.
> They scoff and speak with malice;
>   loftily they threaten oppression.
> They set their mouths against the heavens,
>   and their tongue struts through the earth.
> Therefore his people turn back to them,
>   and find no fault in them.
> And they say, "How can God know?
>   Is there knowledge in the Most High?"
> Behold, these are the wicked;
>   always at ease, they increase in riches.

If the psalmist felt we should "let experience decide," you would expect him to say that he *saw* God judging these people who "set their mouths against the heavens." But no, he *saw* their bodies grow fat and sleek. If you want to "make trial" of God's love allowing "experience to decide," then according to the Bible the verdict will be negative. God's love is not in evidence. God's Word declares this to be the case. Experience to the contrary, the wise Christian will trust in God's gracious purposes and his inscrutable timing, without avoiding or sugar-coating the brutal realities of life.

Solomon has made a confession of faith about God's control over the times (3:1–15), but now he must deal with the fact that his confession is indeed a confession *of faith*. He walks by faith and not by sight, confessing again that "there is a time for every matter and for every work" even though he has yet to *see* the time of judgment. Anyone who has stumbled around in the dark groping for a light switch knows the frustration of being unable to walk by sight. It happens to us when we are driving late at night or early in the morning, when sudden thick fog overwhelms the windshield and we have to slam on the brakes and slow down to a snail's pace. Walking by faith is even more frustrating than groping for a light in a dark room. According to Solomon, there is no light switch in the darkness, but you must make your way by listening to a voice tell you that there is a good reason for the furniture that obstructs your path even though you can detect no pattern to it. Worse, the voice claims it is good for you to bruise your shins even though there is no way to see how the pain could be beneficial.

Solomon will not list aspects of the discrepancy between what he believes and what he sees until the end of chapter 4. Then, in Ecclesiastes 5:1–17, he will offer some advice on how to live with this discrepancy. Here in 3:16–22 he begins with the first two discrepancies that are obvious to anyone who looks around them at what is happening in the world: injustice and death.

In mentioning tyranny and death (or as the contemporary American saying goes, "death and taxes"), Solomon is not listing two unrelated phenomena. Tyrants hold power over us through the threat of death (Heb. 2:14–15). Thus it is natural for Solomon to move from the problem of injustice to the problem of human mortality.

Like the witches chanting "fair is foul and foul is fair" in Shakespeare's *Macbeth*, Solomon fixes his gaze on the hypocrisy of injustice—the fact that it is found precisely where society is supposed to protect the innocent and enforce justice and fairness. God has instituted these human tribunals, these places of judgment so that men could find some justice, some judicial relief from wickedness. When wickedness itself is found there, then it is serious indeed.

Where is this? Where can we find a "place of righteousness"? The most obvious place would be our civil courts. Do you want to disagree with Solomon's observations? Do we usually see the courts of our land as a place where justice and righteousness are defended and preserved? Do we find marriage protected and the unborn defended there?

We should also include our churches. After all, churches are supposed to be places where we find righteousness and even justice (1 Cor. 6:1–8). Do we find this to be the case? The very week I was preaching this text to my own congregation, I heard of yet another pastor who defiled the pastoral office through gross injustice and wickedness, and I have heard of many since. How do you respond to such things? Do you lose hope? What about the home? The family is supposed to be a place of nurture, where righteousness is protected and preserved, but is it? Continually I hear stories of parental abuse that makes me sick to my stomach.

How about our schools? Names like Jonesboro, Arkansas and Columbine High School immediately spring to mind. In 2005, Josh Weise killed five students at Red Lake High School in Minnesota, in addition to a teacher, security guard, his grandfather, and a woman living with him. Our schools are supposed to be places where children are taught, but we find injustice there as well.

How do we typically deal with such injustice? We try to cover it, to gloss over it with a "spiritual" statement. There are all sorts of pious things that we are tempted to say about these situations: "It'll all work out for the best," or, "God has some reason for this." The truth is that not one of us knows how or when or if God will rectify unrighteousness in this life. We don't know why God allows these injustices or, once they have happened, how he could possibly address them in an adequate way that proves his own faithfulness.

How does Solomon respond to this? He responds with a confession: "God shall judge the righteous and the wicked." (3:17) This is an article of faith. You do not learn it from experience. You do not see it in the world around you. Rather, you hear God say it. You hear God tell you that he will bring everything into judgment. And you believe it and confess it because you are certain that God is trustworthy. Judgment belongs to God's time. God will take care of it just as he takes care of what from our perspective is irretrievable—the past!

All of this reminds us of and reiterates what Solomon said at the beginning of chapter 3: "For everything there is a season, and a time for every matter under heaven." All of these seasons and times are God's works and here is another one: a time for unrighteousness and a time for putting things right, a time for injustice and a time for judgment. Here we come close to an empirical observation. Solomon has spoken of the "times" of birth and death, killing and healing, love and hate—all of these times are governed and given by God himself in his good time. They are not subject to man's determination. There were times for reversals and contradictions, for sudden shifts from one thing to its opposite. Now, if anything calls out for a reversal, it is the long winter of misrule and injustice that resides in the places appointed for righteousness. These reversals point to the possibility that tyranny will be reversed too.

Why the delay? What's the point? What is God waiting for? Why is he making us wait? The answer begins in verse eighteen: "I said in my heart with regard to the children of man that God is testing them that they may see that they themselves are but beasts." Our first need is not to teach God his business or to instruct him about the times and seasons when he should act. Rather, our need is to learn the truth about ourselves—that in a very significant way we are not different than the animals. This is a lesson we are slow to accept, but it is not rationally deniable. What happens to us humans is exactly what happens to the animals: we both die and decompose. The breath departs from man and beast alike. Our lives are all mere vapor.

This is no justification for Desmond Morris's famous description of humanity as a "naked ape." Solomon is not saying that man is no more than a highly evolved animal. Rather, mankind has been reduced to the level of dying like animals because of God's judgment. Adam and Eve, according to Genesis 3, thought they might rise to the level of divinity. Instead, they were laid low like the animals:

> [C]ursed is the ground because of you;
> in pain you shall eat of it all the days of your life;
> thorns and thistles it shall bring forth for you;
> and you shall eat the plants of the field.
> By the sweat of your face
> you shall eat bread,
> till you return to the ground,
> for out of it you were taken;
> for you are dust,
> and to dust you shall return.

Death is a message to us—a message that we are finite and limited, that we are not God but are rather answerable to him. God is testing man to see if he will get the point. When you think about Adam and Eve, it is obvious that what God is doing fits the situation. Adam and Eve wanted to exalt themselves by their own efforts in order to become gods, and even though death is a constant reminder that this is not possible, still today many try to deny their place in creation. They insist on imagining that we are somehow in control and that our efforts can and will give us leverage in the world. We die like beasts because we imagine ourselves to be as gods (Gen. 3:17) and we try to pretend we are gods even though we die like beasts. Death is the ultimate evidence of the inexplicable character of God's work and the vaporous nature of our own work.

To repeat, Solomon is *not* saying that animals and men are alike in every respect or that both have the same quality of life; he is reminding us of our mortality. Men are not immortal. They die. The sentence structure in the Hebrew serves to emphasize the fact that men have no advantage over the animals in this matter. Both die. All this is vapor, mist.

Death is the best illustration of our situation. Reader, you and I are going to die. That is the clearest proof that you have no control. You can't control life. You have no power over your destiny. Diet as much as you want. Lift weights as much as you want. When Solomon says that this is all vapor, he is right. Death is the ultimate manifestation of the fact that we are not in control. We have no advantage and no leverage. There are no knobs to turn or switches to pull or buttons to push that will give us control. Technological development doesn't help. The customer at the local electronics store can acquire no gizmo that will deal with death.

Solomon goes further: "All go to one place. All are from the dust, and to dust all return. Who knows whether the spirit of man ['Adam'] goes upward and the spirit of the beast goes down into the earth?" (3:20). The question "who knows," in effect, asserts that nobody has direct first-hand empirical evidence of what happens to the human spirit after death. I know people who attempt to make a case for the biblical afterlife by pointing to stories of near-death experiences, but Solomon doesn't think such evidence is available. Will there be a final solution to the anomaly of injustice and death? Such a resolution lies beyond human verification, beyond empirical testing. When you walk into that funeral parlor, where is the person you once knew? Can you prove that he still exists? That he has been placed somewhere else? Do you have any first-hand evidence? Did you see the soul rise?

In the light of God's unpredictable, uncontrollable activity in the world, Solomon states his conclusion: "So I saw that there is nothing better than that a man should rejoice in his work, for that is his lot. Who can bring him to see what will be after him?" Solomon has said this before, but here we have an addition—a reason is given: "for that is his lot [or portion]." The portion is the inherited lot one has to work on. If God is in control (which has been the strong theme in chapter 3), then our circumstances are our inheritance from God. When you own a piece of property, you have to work and toil on that property, but you get to enjoy it too. The lot is limited. It must be maintained. In light of God's inscrutable working in the world, we cannot worry about the future or other aspects of creation. We must work with what we do have and rejoice in it.

Thus Martin Luther sums it up: "This, then, is the portion of the righteous: to enjoy the things that are present and not be afflicted by the things that are in the future." Hengstenberg agrees: "You are not the master of the future . . . therefore rejoice in the present."

Above I wrote, "Solomon would say that we experience life first as curse, not blessing." The suffering and misery that God has laid upon men speaks of the anger and wrath of God. But some things have changed since Solomon's day. That statement needs to be augmented for the Christian. We can move beyond Solomon since we have the enormous benefit of living after the cross. This still involves walking by faith rather than by sight, but the faith we have is an acceptance of eyewitness testimony that the curse of death has been overturned to resurrection life in the case of Jesus.

Now, with the clarifying manifestation of the cross, we believe—we trust—that the injustice, suffering, and even the death we experience are no longer evidence of God's curse, but of his love, just as they were for the Son of God! We believe this. We confess this, experiences to the contrary. Knowing that we are in Christ, united to Christ, we believe that the injustice and suffering we experience is done in union with Christ. Thus the apostle Paul writes that he suffers loss "that I may know him and the power of his resurrection, and may share his sufferings, becoming like him in his death" (Phil. 3:10). The apostle Peter shared his view: "Beloved, do not be surprised at the fiery trial when it comes upon you to test you, as though something strange were happening to you. But rejoice insofar as you share Christ's sufferings, that you may also rejoice and be glad when his glory is revealed" (1 Pet. 4:12–13).

Do we see injustice in the places of judgment? Have you been the victim of injustice? Was there ever any injustice like that which the gospel writers expose for us in the Roman and Jewish trials of Jesus? God himself suffered the ultimate injustice at the hands of the highest, most respected of human courts. Thus, Peter also wrote:

> For this is a gracious thing, when, mindful of God, one endures sorrows while suffering unjustly. For what credit is it if, when you sin and are beaten for it, you endure? But if when you do good and suffer for it you endure, this is a gracious thing in the sight of God. For to this you have been called, because Christ also suffered for you, leaving you an example, so that you might follow in his steps. He committed no sin, neither was deceit found in his mouth. When he was reviled, he did not revile in return; when he suffered, he did not threaten, but continued entrusting himself to him who judges justly. (1 Pet. 2:19–23)

Do you, in a moment of terror, reflect upon the inevitability of your own death? Do relatives and friends die and return to the dust like animals? We can pretty up the body, of course, and put it in a cushioned coffin. But he or she is no less dead than a deer hit by a car and left at the side of the road. Do we have any empirical evidence of the post-death existence of those who have died? No, we don't. All the New Age books in the world can't change the fact that we have no access to the existence of those who have died.

What we do have is the death and resurrection of the very Son of God. Consider what Paul says: "If in this life only we have hoped in Christ, we are of all people most to be pitied" (1 Cor. 15:19). Our hope is in the resurrection. Paul assures us that "the sufferings of this present time are not worth comparing with the glory that is to be revealed to us" (Rom. 8:18). And so we have assurance:

> Who shall separate us from the love of Christ? Shall tribulation, or distress, or persecution, or famine, or nakedness, or danger, or sword? As it is written, "For your sake we are being killed all the day long; we are regarded as sheep to be slaughtered." No, in all these things we are more than conquerors through him who loved us. (Rom. 8:35–37)

ZERO, ONE, TWO, THREE

I was once told of an old parable from King Charlemagne of a wise father who was about to die. He gathered his sons together and gave them a bundle of sticks to break. They could not break them when they were bundled, but when he unbundled them they were able to break them one by one.

Alone, a man or woman can be broken!

I told this story as I first learned it. Since then I have learned it was actually one of Aesop's fables and was created long before Charlemagne was born. I like Charlemagne as the storyteller because he was a king talking about training sons just like Solomon, so that is the version I told. And the message is virtually identical to what Solomon is teaching us in this portion of Ecclesiastes.

> Again I saw all the oppressions that are done under the sun. And behold, the tears of the oppressed, and they had no one to comfort them! On the side of their oppressors there was power, and there was no one to comfort them. And I thought the dead who are already dead more fortunate than the living who are still alive. But better than both is he who has not yet been and has not seen the evil deeds that are done under the sun.
>
> Then I saw that all toil and all skill in work come from a man's envy of his neighbor. This also is [vapor] and [shepherding the wind].
>
> The fool folds his hands and eats his own flesh.
>
> Better is a handful of quietness than two hands full of toil and [shepherding the wind].
>
> Again, I saw [vapor] under the sun: one person who has no other, either son or brother, yet there is no end to all his toil, and his eyes are never satisfied with riches, so that he never asks, "For whom am I toiling and depriving myself of pleasure?" This also is [vapor] and an unhappy business.
>
> Two are better than one, because they have a good reward for their toil. For if they fall, one will lift up his fellow. But woe to him who is alone when he falls and has not another to lift him up! Again, if two lie together, they keep warm, but how can one keep warm alone? And though a man might prevail against one who is alone, two will withstand him—a threefold cord is not quickly broken.
>
> Better was a poor and wise youth than an old and foolish king who no longer knew how to take advice. For he went from prison to the throne, though in his own kingdom he had been born poor. I saw all the living who move about under the sun, along with that youth who was to stand in the king's place. There was no end of all the people, all of whom he led. Yet those who come later will not rejoice in him. Surely this also is [vapor] and [shepherding the wind]. (Eccl. 4)

One helpful way to understand this passage is to see it as inspired arithmetic—sort of like the hit song "One is the Loneliest Number." In verses one through three of chapter 4, zero is better than one. Then, in verses four through six, we read that one is better than two. Climactically, in verses seven through twelve we find that two are better than one. Finally, Solomon stops his math and tells us of a king who wouldn't take advice. With thousands of followers but without advisors, he found himself chasing the wind. Despite the various math sentences, Solomon's ultimate point is that two is better than one and three is better still. Human community is a true gift from God that should be valued.

Chapter 3 ends with the statement that there is "nothing better" than that a man should rejoice in his own works, for that is his "heritage" or "portion" (3:22). But now Solomon immediately proceeds to fill this out. Is this enjoyment, this eating and drinking (2:24–26), an individualistic pursuit—a solitary activity? No. In this section, therefore, Solomon gives his advice to eat, drink, and enjoy life a very concrete shape. *Enjoy these with or in the community of the faithful.* Have a drink with friends. Eat with someone else. Work as part of and for the community. The bond of community is not easily broken. This would all apply especially to the ritual, festival meals of Israel.

Solomon begins by reconsidering political oppression. Indeed, some commentators analyze this text by including 4:1–3 with the previous chapter's mention of tyranny. But Solomon is now looking at this problem from a new angle, an angle that occupies him for this whole chapter. Solomon's angle here is the same one that we see in the gospels in the garden of Gethsemane. Jesus, we find, not only suffers, but he suffers alone while his best friends fall asleep and then abandon him. Solomon gives us two witnesses to testify on his emphasis in this passage, repeating twice, "and there was no one to comfort them." Solomon finds that suffering injustice is much worse when one must do it all alone. Those who have been released from oppression by death have a relative advantage over those who are living under the oppression. At least they are finished with the torment of tyranny! Solomon's concern is not so much to expose oppression so as to stop it; but to expose the brutal reality of a world where injustice is found and in which there is no one to help.

The approach Solomon is taking shows that he does indeed believe that there are real joys and advantages in this life. Specifically, in the midst of vaporous toil and limitations, there is the comfort of human companionship. Throughout history men and women have banded together against tyrants. This is not only because of the idea of safety in numbers, but also because those suffering under oppression want the comfort of fellowship with those who can sympathize.

This leads Solomon to a conclusion that strikes many readers as impious. The pain of human oppression is so acute that one must conclude that those who undergo such torture *alone* would be better off never having lived. If only they would have been spared such a life! As shocking as it seems the Bible shows us other saints making the same statement. When Satan convinced God to destroy Job and isolate him from his own wife and everyone else, rather than curse God, the righteous Job cursed the day of his birth (Job 3). When faced with persecution and isolation, Jeremiah also wishes he had never been born (Jer. 20:14–18). Thus begins Solomon's mathematical literary device: "better than both is he who has not yet been and has not seen the evil deeds that are done under the sun." Zero is better than one. One is the loneliest number that you ever heard.

For his second observation, Solomon moves from the harm inflicted by tyrants to the harm we inflict on ourselves. What Solomon discusses in verses four and five has mainly to do with the one who works and toils to set himself apart from others. He notes what we all know: that so much of what is accomplished is motivated by rivalry or envy. *This is the antithesis of true community and companionship.* If Solomon will say in general that our labor is vapor and a futile attempt to herd the wind, how much more of *this* sort of labor! (4:4b). If companionship is a true good, then labor that alienates oneself can only impoverish no matter what the material gain may be.

On the opposite end of the spectrum is the "fool" who sits alone and lives in a perpetual state of "hand-folding." Thus, in this situation, zero is not good, but neither is a number too large. One is better than two or zero: "Better is a handful of quietness than two hands full of toil and shepherding the wind." Notice that the "quietness" is not inactivity, but reasonable and reasonably-motivated labor (in contrast with the lazy fool). What we see here is that "toil and skill" and "quietness" are not absolute values. They are relative. Work is good if it is done appropriately in a fitting way. Rest is good, too, if enjoyed fittingly. This is the consistent testimony of Scripture: "Better is a little with the fear of the Lord than great treasure and trouble without it" (Prov. 15:16); "There is great gain in godliness with contentment" (1 Tim. 6:6).

Why work yourself to death to set your solitary self apart from everyone else? Be happy with what you have.

Yet Solomon knows that this must be qualified, so he writes his next and third observation. Solomon observes a man who works only for himself. He has no one to help or, more importantly, to work for. He has no one to serve. Solomon seems to be affirming the significance and value of work, but only when there is someone for whose sake you are working.

This section has to do with the significance or value of one man's work. Without someone to serve—literally, "without a second" (Eccl. 4:8a)—it is just vapor from beginning to end. Thus, this observation (4:7–8) begins and ends with "vapor." The word "one" is used three times in this verse to emphasis the solitude of the individual. This solitary individual relentlessly pursues riches and he is never satisfied with his current accumulation. This solitary worker never even stops to ask about the purpose of his hard work: Who will actually benefit from my toil?

Jesus agreed with Solomon: "For whoever would save his life will lose it, but whoever loses his life for my sake and the gospel's will save it. For what does it profit a man to gain the whole world and forfeit his life?" (Mark 8:35–36). Remember the context of Jesus's words. He is telling of his own service, his own dedication to give his life for his disciples.

Here Solomon makes his final mathematical statement: two is better than one . . . but three is better still! Two is better than one because now some purpose, some reason, appears for working. The point of laboring is to share what one gains with another. The two also provide mutual assistance to one another. They have a "good reward" for their mutual labor. Now Solomon gives us a rare instance of some relative "advantage" or "leverage" or "profit" in human life. It concerns our loving work for another. This is quite a different rationale for work than the one offered in 4:4–6. Working for oneself is vapor but working for others is a great gain. Work has meaning primarily as a way of expressing love, not as a means of accumulating individual wealth.

This conclusion (Eccl. 4:9–12) represents the climax of the passage. Solomon signifies this by making it longer than any of his partial conclusions earlier in this chapter. Instead of stopping in verse nine, he extends his description of the two and their advantage in contrast with the mere one.

Solomon offers three self-evident reasons why two are better than one by giving us three if-clauses. Then he surprises us with a new conclusion: "a threefold cord is not quickly broken."

Unfortunately, this saying has taken on a sentimental, romantic life of its own in modern wedding ceremonies, where it is interpreted to refer to husband and wife and God (a threefold cord). This is almost surely *not* the meaning of the aphorism. It might seem pious to bring God into the three, but it is surely Solomon's purpose to praise *human* companionship under the sun.

As was so marvelously presented in the British movie *About a Boy*, even two can be vulnerable. They need "back-up." Two friends can be of great help to one another, but if one is dead or rendered permanently helpless then all that is left is one trying to cover both sets of needs. The importance of life and long-term-care insurance for married couples is a testament to the need for people to help one another. In the Bible, one reason children are considered a blessing is because once they have grown, they can add to the support structure. If two are helpful, then three is *not* a crowd. Three is a *community*.

Readers need to remember that God created man as a family in order to make them in the divine image (Gen. 1:27). Looking back on Solomon's statement with New Testament hindsight, it seems that the third actualizes the fullness of social life as in the Trinity. I'm not suggesting something silly, as if Solomon were referring to the Trinity here. What I *am* suggesting is that, in the context of the whole Bible, we who know that God exists as the perfect fullness of social being—the three in one—can understand that a human society of two is not the perfect image of the triune life. Augustine makes this a major plank in his exposition of the Trinity.

This chapter, therefore, praises companionship. It is right that it should culminate with a proverbial saying about the relative goodness of community—that three are even better than a couple. Companionship, whether in the face of oppression (4:1–3) or as providing the meaning and purpose for hard work (4:4–9) or in life generally (4:10–12), is better than solitude and may serve to redeem partially an otherwise intolerable vapor-existence under the sun by injecting into it some meaning and purpose. The thrust of this section seems to be that we are in a world burdened by oppression, injustice, exhausting work, falling down cold, and being knocked down. To face such a life with companionship is decidedly better than to do so alone. In fact, non-existence or death is often preferable to the curse of solitude.

Chapter 4 ends with a warning to leaders, whether businessmen, politicians, or pastors. Being a leader of a multitude is no substitute for being involved in a real community of peers. While there is some debate as to what is said about the "poor and wise youth" and the "old and foolish king" (4:13), it is clear that if you are in a position without trusted friends who can give advice, your labor will be vapor no matter how popular a leader you are. Popularity is not the same as community or fellowship.

The reformer Martin Luther summarized this chapter well. "The meaning is: It is better to be in association with others and to enjoy things in common than to be a solitary miser who only cares about himself and grabs things for himself alone. In society there is mutual help, common work, [and] common solace" (*Luther's Works*, 15 [Concordia], 69).

Perhaps it would be helpful to make some systematic application of Solomon's teaching. We can see the importance of Solomon's teaching if we set it in the context of several wider Biblical concerns.

(1) The estate of solitude, of being alone, is one of the miseries of this life that man brought upon himself at the fall. It was not God's intention to create man without intimate fellowship and community. We have God's assurance that "it is not good for man to be alone" (Gen. 2:18). Adam and Eve's fall into sin was a breach of the interpersonal covenant between them, and, by implication, of every hu-

man relationship. God acted in judgment not only to cause enmity between the two seeds of the woman, but also to deal with rivalry and dissention between husband and wife (Gen. 3:16). We see the social devastation of sin moving swiftly in the first five chapters of Genesis into the brother-brother relationship (Gen. 4) and then into the whole of human society. The curse of sin, the burden laid upon the sons of Adam, to use the language of Ecclesiastes, is the frustration and the helplessness of solitude and alienation from our fellow human beings. Hell is often depicted as hyper-individualism.

(2) All the gospels show us quite clearly how Jesus suffered from solitude as part of his work on the cross. This was his chosen task. This was part of bearing the burden of the curse for us. All his disciples forsook him so he was utterly alone in those last hours of darkness and torment. He was alone on the cross, alienated both from his Father *and* from his brother and sisters.

(3) An essential part of salvation is the restoration of community and of genuine companionship. Alienation from God entails alienation in the created realm, so restoration to God must be correlative with restoration with other men and women. We are incorporated into a society when we are saved—into a new humanity, which is the body of Christ, the church. There is really no such thing as isolated saved individuals (if it happens, it is only in extremely unusual circumstances).

(4) The members of the body of Christ who are more blessed in this regard are responsible to be careful to incorporate those members that are particularly susceptible to the ravages of alienation and solitude. Widows, orphans, and foreigners are always singled out as those to whom the church must pay special attention. Congregations need to be specially attentive to divorcées in their midst, singles, college students far away from their families, and international students. Those who are aged or infirm also need to be included in the life of the body. When we make efforts to include such people in community life in a sincere and non-patronizing way, we image our God who put us in a new family. "Sing to God, sing praises to his name; lift up a song to him who rides through the deserts; his name is the Yahweh; exult before him! Father of the fatherless and protec-

tor of widows is God in his holy habitation. God settles the solitary in a home; he leads out the prisoners to prosperity, but the rebellious dwell in a parched land" (Ps. 68:4–6). James agrees with the psalmist: "Religion that is pure and undefiled before God, the Father, is this: to visit orphans and widows in their affliction, and to keep oneself unstained from the world" (Jas. 1:27).

Here, then, is true religion—genuine holiness and righteousness before God. It not only involves providing for obvious material needs, but genuine friendship and companionship. Extending such friendship requires effort, but it is what God requires. It is also what God blesses. Statistics show that if new members of a church do not find genuine companionship within a year, they will leave.

Of course, it works both ways. Personally, both as a layman and then a pastor, I have noticed in church after church that too many of those people that leave have made no effort themselves to find friendship. We may think good preaching or exalting worship is what draws us to a church. Our culture may train us not to consider the issue of alienation and fellowship. When we do not become genuine members of a real fellowship, we will grow restless and dissatisfied. Solomon's wisdom should raise our awareness of the importance of communion with the body of Christ and the foolishness of "not neglecting to meet together, as is the habit of some, but encouraging one another, and all the more as you see the Day drawing near" (Heb. 10:25).

7

HOUSEHOLD ETIQUETTE: ECCLESIASTES 5:1–20

I am writing these things to you so that . . . you may know how one ought to behave in the household of God. . . . But those who desire to be rich fall into temptation, into a snare, into many senseless and harmful desires that plunge people into ruin and destruction.
—1 Timothy 3:15–16; 6:9

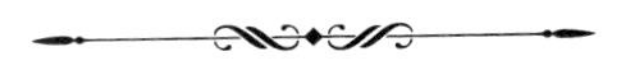

"Children should be seen and not heard." I don't know how many times I heard that as a child from my mother when we went to parties or out to eat. Or, when adults were speaking, "Listen and don't interrupt." Do we still give our children those kinds of admonitions?

You see, it is crucial for a child to learn his or her *place*, to learn what kind of behavior is appropriate for him or her as a child. One of the most important ways in which children show that they know their place is the way they control their tongues. The same is true of adults. We all have a place, a station in life. And Solomon's wisdom here has to do with the Christian's appropriate verbal behavior given his or her place.

To some extent our society seems to have forgotten the importance of knowing our place. It is not often taught to our children. However, there is something else that becomes evident in this portion of Ecclesiastes that is even farther removed from today's culture. Solomon is not only concerned that we know our place, but also that we especially show that we do so when we are in a special place—the house of God. To understand why Solomon has such concerns we need to review the Biblical world model of Solomon's day as well as that of Christians today.

> Guard your steps when you go to the house of God. To draw near to listen is better than to offer the sacrifice of fools, for they do not know that they are doing evil. Be not rash with your mouth, nor let your heart be hasty to utter a word before God, for God is in heaven and you are on earth. Therefore let your words be few. For a dream comes with much business, and a fool's voice with many words.
>
> When you vow a vow to God, do not delay paying it, for he has no pleasure in fools. Pay what you vow. It is better that you should not vow than that you should vow and not pay. Let not your mouth lead you into sin, and do not say before the messenger that it was a mistake. Why should God be angry at your voice and destroy the work of your hands? For when dreams increase and words grow many, there is [vapor]; but God is the one you must fear. (Eccl. 5:1–7)

Solomon was the builder of God's temple. What was so significant about God's temple? The answer goes back to Genesis chapters 1 and 2. After the story of the general creation in chapter 1, we have it retold with additional information. God didn't just create "the whole world" in general, as if he made no distinctions. Rather, he made a special land situated among other lands. In this special land he placed man along with many trees including two special ones. This land and sanctuary was in a very high place, for four major rivers flowed from it to the other lands. It was what happened in this special place that cursed the entire creation. When Adam and Eve sinned by trespassing and stealing restricted food, they were exiled from the sanctuary Garden and a cherub was put there to guard the way to the Tree of Life with his flaming sword (Gen. 3).

The main point here is that when God told Moses to build a tent for him—called a tabernacle—he was not doing something entirely new. After all, Moses was leading God's chosen people out of Egypt across the wilderness into a new special land in the midst of the nations. On the way there he had them build a new sanctuary to be in this special land. This sanctuary has architectural trees and fruit (Ex. 25:33, 34; 28:33; 39:24, 15; 37:19, 20). There were also cherubim in both tapestry and sculpture present there (Ex. 25:18–22; 26:1, 31, etc.). The tabernacle sanctuary, to sum up, was a new garden sanctuary. By establishing his people in a special land with a special sanctuary, God was re-establishing the edenic order. Solomon's temple, built centuries later, was much more glorious, but it too was filled with tree and angel references in the architecture.

There are many other correlations that could be pointed out. For example, not only did the garden correspond to the tabernacle, but also Adam in the Garden corresponds to the priests serving in the tabernacle. We are told of Adam, "The LORD God took the man and put him in the Garden of Eden to *serve* it and *guard* it" (Gen. 2:8). In the entire five books of Moses, those two words are found together only once: "And you and your sons with you shall *guard* your priesthood for all that concerns the altar and that is within the veil; and you shall *serve*. I give your priesthood as a gift, and any outsider who comes near shall be put to death" (Num. 18:7).

God cared not only about a tent or a building. The sanctuary was a way of designating *a people* to be near him. His point in somehow dwelling at the sanctuary was to gather a people to himself to serve him (1 Pet. 2:4–10). And just as disobedience in the sanctuary in the special land resulted in worldwide destruction, so a trespass among the sanctuary people resulted in worldwide destruction. Instead of listing many examples, we can see this simply by finding the principle articulated by the prophet Asa:

> For a long time Israel was without the true God, and without a teaching priest and without law, but when in their distress they turned to the LORD, the God of Israel, and sought him, he was found by them. In those times there was no peace to him who went out or to him who came in, for great disturbances afflicted all the inhabitants of the lands. They were broken in pieces. Nation was crushed by nation and city by city, for God troubled them with every sort of distress. (2 Chron. 15:3–6)

What happens in the sanctuary land, what is done by the sanctuary people, has incredible consequences for the whole world. When Jesus came to the sanctuary people, he showed just this sort of concern.

> You are the salt of the earth, but if salt has lost its taste, how shall its saltiness be restored? It is no longer good for anything except to be thrown out and trampled under people's feet. You are the light of the world. A city set on a hill cannot be hidden. Nor do people light a lamp and put it under a basket, but on a stand, and it gives light to all in the house. In the same way, let your light shine before others, so that they may see your good works and give glory to your Father who is in heaven. (Matt. 5:13–16)

We are the ones who are supposed to make the world taste acceptable to God (Lev. 2:13; Num. 18:19) and to illuminate it. Corporately, the church is the fulfillment of the tabernacle and temple (Eph. 2:19–22; 1 Cor. 3:9–17; 1 Pet. 2:4–10). While we no longer have only one sanctuary, we still "come together as a church" (1 Cor. 11:18) to be standing in God's special presence. While it is true that God in Christ is present by the Spirit with believers in every place and at every time, it remains true that there is a special way God is present with us in worship. Otherwise, Jesus would be speaking nonsense when he promises that "where two or three are gathered in my name, there am I among them" (Matt. 18:20). When we gather for worship and, to an extent, simply when we gather with and interact with local Christians, we are in God's special presence as his special people. While the fulfillment of the full gospel story means that we have a greater understanding of the love of God and a greater reason for joy, the New Testament indicates we also have a greater reason for fear and trembling than Solomon did.

> For you have not come to what may be touched, a blazing fire and darkness and gloom and a tempest and the sound of a trumpet and a voice whose words made the hearers beg that no further messages be spoken to them. For they could not endure the order that was given, "If even a beast touches the mountain, it shall be stoned." Indeed, so terrifying was the sight that Moses said, "I tremble with fear." But you have come to Mount Zion and to the city of the living God, the heavenly Jerusalem, and to innumerable angels in festal gathering, and to the assembly of the firstborn who are enrolled in heaven, and to God, the judge of all, and to the spirits of the righteous made perfect, and to Jesus, the mediator of a new covenant, and to the sprinkled blood that speaks a better word than the blood of Abel. (Heb. 12:18–24)

Church and worship are important, but what particular sin is Solomon concerned might be committed in the church or in worship?

Do you know your place before God? Among the people of God? Your words will tell the true story. Your words will justify or vindicate you. Jesus tells us that "wisdom is justified by her children" (Matt. 11:19). Your children are your words. You bring them forth. They are the fruit of your heart. Jesus, after all, also solemnly warned his disciples, "The good person out of his good treasure brings forth good, and the evil person out of his evil treasure brings forth evil. I tell you, on the day of judgment people will give account for every careless word they speak, for by your words you will be justified, and by your words you will be condemned" (Matt. 12:35–37).

Strong stuff, yet Jesus did not invent the concept. He had a lot of precedent in the Hebrew Scriptures. Jesus's warning is uttered in conjunction with everything the Lord had already said in the Old Testament about careless, foolish talk.

Ecclesiastes 5 is a pivotal passage. This is not accidental. Solomon is not randomly collecting moralistic advice. Rather, it follows from his previous statements about the need for human companionship and the foolishness of alienating oneself from others for an imagined gain that only turns out to be vapor. Without godly speech with humility in words and tone, human community will not last a minute. It would be only too easy to fill pages showing how the apostle Paul was concerned that the churches be built up and not torn down by means of human speech. Furthermore, in the theme of the whole book of Ecclesiastes, Solomon has emphasized how our toil and labor gives us no advantage or leverage. It is all *vapor*. Now we are seeing why such a perspective, far from being cynical or ungodly, is actually a key to true piety in speech. It is precisely because we presume our words mean so much and are so important that we are easily tempted to sin with our tongues.

In this section Solomon warns against incautious speech in the presence of God among his people. The passage consists of four admonitions.

5:1 Guard your steps.
5:2 Do not be quick with your mouth.
5:4 When you make a vow, do not delay in fulfilling it.
5:6 Do not let your mouth lead you into sin.

These four admonitions are distributed pretty evenly between two basic subjects. First (5:1–3), Solomon cautions against all forms of hasty speech in the house of God. Second (5:4–7), there is a specific form of speech before God that demands heightened caution—that is, the vow made to the Lord to perform some promise.

Both of these concerns have to do with our speech in the house of God (5:2). Solomon is warning against the kind of mistakes that a fool makes in worship or among God's assembled people in the sanctuary. The fool is especially prone to incautious speech in such contexts. Solomon is saying, to retranslate slightly, "Walk prudently when you go to the house of God; and draw near to hear rather than to give the sacrifice of fools." The opposite of hearing or listening is talking. "The sacrifice of fools," here, is a negative version of offering up "a sacrifice of praise to God, that is, the fruit of lips that acknowledge his name" (Heb. 13:15). The fool's sacrifice, in this context, is an offering of words—words hastily uttered before God. Be not rash with your mouth, nor let your heart be hasty to utter a word before God (Eccl. 5:2). More literally the text reads "do not let your heart rush to bring up a matter in God's presence."

Few words are one of the indelible signs of the wise, for they speak only after sufficient reflection (Prov. 10:14, 19; Jas. 1:19). Our speech ought to be constrained and tempered when we are among God's people, but in fact it is often precisely the opposite that takes place. Being among God's people is coming into God's presence. Even in a small gathering this is true. After all, Jesus promised to be present even when only two or three are gathered in his name. Fools do not realize the significance of God's presence.

One of the signs of a fool is found in someone who talks too much. I don't necessarily mean someone who talks a great deal (gregariousness is not to be equated with foolishness). Rather, it is a sign of foolishness to talk too much about people, things, and matters that don't properly concern them.

> When words are many, transgression is not lacking,
> but whoever restrains his lips is prudent. (Prov. 10:19)
>
> Whoever keeps his mouth and his tongue
> keeps himself out of trouble. (Prov. 21:23)
>
> Whoever restrains his words has knowledge,
> and he who has a cool spirit is a man of
> understanding. (Prov. 17:27)
>
> Even a fool who keeps silent is considered wise;
> when he closes his lips, he is deemed intelligent. (Prov. 17:28)

Do you always have something to say? Do you ever listen to people? Or do you just wait for an opportunity to say something, always formulating in your mind what you will say without listening carefully? "Know this, my beloved brothers: let every person be quick to hear, slow to speak, slow to anger" (Jas. 1:19).

Solomon does not identify the precise kind of speech he is referring to, but the qualifying statements in these first few verses indicate that he is talking about our speech in the house of God

(5:1, 2, "before God," and 6). His warning is sufficiently ambiguous to encompass every word we utter in God's presence. We need to ask, however, what kind of words—hasty words—we are likely to utter among God's people. What kind of verbal sins are we prone to commit in the assembly of the saints?

Solomon is probably referring to *hasty judgments* made in God's presence. The sacrifice of fools is an offering of words similar to the words of the Israelite leader in the temple as Jesus tells the story in Luke 18:9–14. In God's presence the man says, "O God, I thank you that I am not like these other men, especially this unholy, compromised man next to me. I am holy and pure and theologically correct." And so out of his mouth comes the offering to God of a fool, words that were better left unsaid. This man doesn't know his place. God is in heaven and this man is on earth. He talks too much.

For some people, going to church is like going to an ecclesiastical home improvement warehouse. They just love to shop for lumber. And it's always in someone else's eye. "Why do you see the speck that is in your brother's eye, but do not notice the log that is in your own eye? Or how can you say to your brother, 'Let me take the speck out of your eye,' when there is the log in your own eye? You hypocrite, first take the log out of your own eye, and then you will see clearly to take the speck out of your brother's eye" (Matt. 7:3–5).

Almost the entire substance of church gossip—foolish speech—can be reduced to hasty, uncharitable judgments against other people in the church. "For lack of wood the fire goes out, and where there is no whisperer, quarreling ceases" (Prov. 26:20). "Whoever goes about slandering reveals secrets, but he who is trustworthy in spirit keeps a thing covered" (Prov. 11:13). If you know something unseemly about a person, if you have some knowledge of some sin, then it would be wiser to conceal it than to get on the phone with someone else. No matter how much you powder up your talebearing with the aromatic assurances of pious and holy motivations, to God it smells like the speech of a fool.

Remember your calling. Remember your place. It is not your station in life to pass judgment on everyone else in your church. "Who are you to pass judgment on the servant of another? It is before his own master that he stands or falls. And he will be upheld, for the Lord is able to make him stand . . . Why do you pass judgment on your brother? Or you, why do you despise your brother? For we will all stand before the judgment seat of God" (Rom. 14:4, 10).

It is true that God allows for judgment in the church. He has placed pastors and other authorities in local churches, but such an office is fraught with difficulties. In the church there are not many masters—not many teachers. "Not many of you should become teachers, my brothers, for you know that we who teach will be judged with greater strictness" (Jas. 3:1). James immediately goes on to warn about the sins of lips. It is quite tempting for us to judge others, but when we do so we are arrogating to ourselves an office we have not been given.

Some people think that their own spirituality is heightened and elevated according to how well and how often they point out the faults of others, but the Bible indicates the opposite is true. Rather, spirituality is measured according to your ability to restore an offender. In much of evangelical culture, one would deduce that Galatians 6:1 says "Brothers, if anyone is caught in any transgression, you who are spiritual should get on the phone and tell everyone about it, and, most of all, how much it shocks you, since you are so pure and holy." That's not what it says. "Brothers, if anyone is caught in any transgression, you who are spiritual should restore him in a spirit of gentleness." Despite such clear instructions, the talebearer never appears to be a fool—especially to himself. He is always so concerned, so self-righteously concerned, about the church or the person involved. Solomon's wisdom cuts through this disguise, both in Ecclesiastes and in his other writings: "Whoever hates disguises himself with his lips and harbors deceit in his heart; when he speaks graciously, believe him not, for there are seven abominations in his heart" (Prov. 26:24–25).

In fact, the fool even fools himself. "To draw near to listen is better than to offer the sacrifice of fools, *for they do not know that they are doing evil*" (Eccl. 5:1). The problem with the fool in cases like this is that they don't think they are fools, but truly believe that they are wise. That's why they talk so much. While everyone else can usually see it, the person himself cannot. In fact, this is a good time to test yourself. You might be thinking right now of someone else who fits this bill. Could it be you? It is particularly hard for the man or woman who habitually speaks hastily to have the discernment to judge himself. They are in the habit of judging others, but of excusing themselves. This is the kind of incautious, hasty speech that has no part among God's people, in God's house (Ps. 15:1–3).

There is a second kind of foolish verbal sacrifice that we often offer to God in the presence of his people. For lack of a better way to put it, I will call it the sacrifice of "*look-at-how-pious-I-am* radical resolutions." Peter does this, you will remember, in the presence of the Lord on the night of his arrest, insisting that he is so loyal that he will never deny Jesus (Matt. 26:30–35). Those words will come back to bite him.

While there are many examples of this, I have been dismayed by this kind of talk particularly among young parents who are eager to set themselves apart as more holy than those parents who have older children. The verbal offering of look-at-how-pious-I-am radical resolutions comes too easily to their lips. Beware of the words *never* and *always*.

"I'll never send my children to day care."
"I'll never put my children in a public school."
"Well, I will never allow my teenagers to do such and such."
"I'll always homeschool my children."

These are easy words to utter when your children are very small. Despite being easy, the ones who make them often act as if making them is some great deed on their part. These are pompous, holier-than-thou, look-at-how-radically-committed-I-am words.

Wise men and women, Christians who guard their steps, don't make foolish promises like that. These are words that you may one day have to eat. Such words are evidence of foolish dreaming, not sober self-evaluation. "Therefore let your words be few. For a dream comes with much business, and a fool's voice with many words . . . For when dreams increase and words grow many, there is vapor; but God is the one you must fear" (Eccl. 5:3). It is always easier to be courageously obedient in your own mind than it is to do what you are required to do right now. It is easier to boast about tomorrow than it is to show humility in the present.

> Come now, you who say, "Today or tomorrow we will go into such and such a town and spend a year there and trade and make a profit"—yet you do not know what tomorrow will bring. What is your life? For you are a mist that appears for a little time and then vanishes. Instead you ought to say, "If the Lord wills, we will live and do this or that." As it is, you boast in your arrogance. All such boasting is evil. So whoever knows the right thing to do and fails to do it, for him it is sin. (Jas. 4:13–17)

Certain tasks require large amounts of work to perform. When people dream of great accomplishments, they often fail to realize how much disciplined and strenuous action will be required. So the dream remains a foolish, unrealized dream. In the same way the "voice of a fool" is associated with a lot of talking, but with little or no action. Too much talk is as fruitless as too much dreaming.

This kind of arrogant, self-serving speech is not confined, of course, to mothers and fathers, but occurs in the church whenever we want to set ourselves apart from someone else as more pious and committed. We accomplish this by making some sort of promise about the future which we subsequently and conveniently forget when the future finally gets here. Your life is a mist; your life is a [vapor]. So let your words be appropriate rather than the sacrifice of fools.

The third kind of verbal sacrifice of fools, related to the second one, but more grievous, is the vow that is taken to God but then not fulfilled (Eccl. 5:4–7). The vow made to God, under these circumstances, is merely a formalizing or ceremonializing of a *look-at-how-pious-I-am* radical resolution.

A vow or oath is a solemn promise made to God, and men are witnesses. It is a personal commitment to God to perform some duty taken in the presence of witnesses. While the spontaneous making of vows isn't common in evangelical circles, there are various vows that are an important part of life. People make vows, typically, when becoming *members* of a local congregation. They vow to support the church and be faithful in attendance. How often do Christians actually strive to be faithful to those vows? Another vow is baptism. Whether one realizes or not, being baptized places one under a solemn oath to trust God and be faithful to the gospel. How often do we find people, perhaps either at college or during a midlife crisis, throwing off the yoke of their baptismal vow and abandoning the faith? Church office involves a vow to fulfill the duties of that office, yet we hear of pastors leaving their posts all the time, often due to scandalous sin. Marriage vows are commonly made but not commonly honored. All of these vows are made voluntarily and under no compulsion from an external authority.

Vows in the Bible can be undertaken for various reasons, but whenever and for whatever reason you utter a vow before God, it must be fulfilled. This includes vows that are uttered when we are in trouble. How much more this applies to those that have been carefully entered into! "I will come into your house with burnt offerings; I will perform my vows to you, that which my lips uttered and my mouth promised when I was in trouble" (Ps. 66:13–14). Christians need to think about what they are saying. Better not to vow than to vow and not fulfill it (Eccl. 5:5). "Make your vows to the LORD your God and perform them; let all around him bring gifts to him who is to be feared" (Ps. 76:11). Think first about your ability to complete a vow before taking it upon yourself. Better to have fewer pastors, fewer elders in the church, fewer deacons, even to have fewer church members, and to have the vows taken really mean something.

When Solomon writes, "do not say before the messenger that it was a mistake" (Eccl. 5:6), he is referring to the temple messenger who would be the priest or Levite before whom the person has made his vow. He comes to ask why you haven't done what you promised! Now, at a later date, the man who took the rash vow must confess to the priest or pastor that his vow was made by mistake. The Hebrew word for "mistake" here is always used in the sense of an inadvertent error. It was unintentional and unpremeditated. The meaning of that word is established in Leviticus and Numbers when appropriate sacrifices are required for inadvertent sins, that is, sins that were not committed with a high hand. Notice that even though inadvertent, being unable to fulfill such a vow is a sin and must be dealt with. It is a very risky prospect: God will be angry with you and destroy the work of your hands! (5:6).

The salient characteristic of the life of the Christian in response to God's gratuitous mercy in Christ ought to be a recognition of our humble place before Almighty God. "For when dreams increase and words grow many, there is [vapor]; but God is the one you must fear" (5:7). The Christian's speech affords the most pointed manifestation of his humble reverence before God. It is the responsibility of Christians to be the kind of persons whose word can be believed and relied upon—normally without the need for swearing and oaths (Matt. 5:33–37). But when solemn witnesses are called for and when God is invoked as the primary witness in vows of church membership or ordination or baptism or marriage, how much more does the Christian pledge himself to absolute obligation?

Do you fear God? Your words will vindicate you or condemn you. Be wise. Watch what you say in God's house and world.

EVEN THOUGH WE AIN'T GOT MONEY

What do you and your wife or your husband fight about the most? What do you remember your parents arguing about when you were growing up? I would guess that more often than not, when a couple fights, they fight over money. I suspect in most cases this is the most common source of contention in marriages by a large margin. The budget, whether or not to strive for a better salary, what to sacrifice and how to use the credit cards, are things that cause a great deal of conflict. This is true not only of marriages but among people all over the world. All of the strife, contention, lawsuits, quarrels, and wars in this world arise from one simple cause—the insatiable desire to acquire more. This was as true thousands of years ago as it is today: "What causes quarrels and what causes fights among you? Is it not this, that your passions are at war within you? You desire and do not have, so you murder. You covet and cannot obtain, so you fight and quarrel. You do not have, because you do not ask" (Jas. 4:1–2).

Remember those days when you actually said to each other that it didn't matter how much money you had? When you sang that Loggins and Messina song and really meant it? "Even though we ain't got money, I'm so in love with you, honey." In most cases that kind of romanticism does not last. And when you are so absorbed, so preoccupied with what you don't have, with what you think you ought to have, and with comparing yourself to someone who has more, isn't it remarkable how blind you become to everything else that really makes the marriage special? The old saying is right—you can blot out the sun if you hold a penny close enough to your eye.

The key, then, is to keep the penny in your pocket and stop staring at it! It is all a matter of perspective, or, as Jesus put it: "For where your treasure is, there your heart will be also" (Matt. 6:21). Solomon has been emphasizing in this section (Eccl. 3–5) our need to learn our place and cultivate the outlook that is appropriate for our lot in life. We need to develop the right outlook for the various times in our lives (chapter 3), for our place within our communities (chapter 4), and our place in God's house as people who speak in his presence (5:1–8). Finally, Solomon concludes this section by goading us to think about our place in life with respect to money.

> If you see in a province the oppression of the poor and the violation of justice and righteousness, do not be amazed at the matter, for an arrogant one watches over another arrogant one, and even more arrogant ones are watching over them. Moreover the profit of the land is for all; even the king is served from the field.
>
> He who loves money will not be satisfied with money, nor he who loves wealth with his income; this also is [vapor]. When goods increase, they increase who eat them, and what advantage has their owner but to see them with his eyes? Sweet is the sleep of a laborer, whether he eats little or much, but the full stomach of the rich will not let him sleep.
>
> There is a grievous evil that I have seen under the sun: riches were kept by their owner to his hurt, and those riches were lost in

> a bad venture. And he is father of a son, but he has nothing in his hand. As he came from his mother's womb he shall go again, naked as he came, and shall take nothing for his toil that he may carry away in his hand. This also is a grievous evil: just as he came, so shall he go, and what gain is there to him who toils for the wind? Moreover, all his days he eats in darkness in much vexation and sickness and anger.
>
> Behold, what I have seen to be good and fitting is to eat and drink and find enjoyment in all the toil with which one toils under the sun the few days of his life that God has given him, for this is his lot. Everyone also to whom God has given wealth and possessions and power to enjoy them, and to accept his lot and rejoice in his toil—this is the gift of God. For he will not much remember the days of his life because God keeps him occupied with joy in his heart. (Eccl. 5:8–20)

He begins (5:8–9) by pointing out rather bluntly that *there will always be someone with more money than you have*—someone who may use it against you. This is a notoriously difficult Hebrew passage to decipher. Even if we cannot be sure about how to translate every detail, the overall meaning is not to difficult to discern. The surprising thing about Solomon's wisdom here is that he says, in effect, "get used to it" or "don't marvel at the matter." The idea is don't be shocked.

Solomon emphasizes economic inequities. The oppressed are the "poor." The Hebrew word for "violent perversion" or "violation" normally indicates "robbery, extortion, and usury." The Hebrew will not really support the idea that these are officials in some sort of bureaucratic governmental system. Rather, these are the "haughty and ambitious" people who think that they can achieve anything they want at other people's expense. These people are driven by envy to do whatever they can to get ahead (4:4–6). Solomon links oppression with ambition and greed. The problem is the insatiable appetite of the haughty rich. Wealth itself is not the problem, but the insatiable longing of those who love money. Commentator Choon-Leon Seow explains the passage's meaning. "The point is that there are such haughty and lofty people everywhere trying to climb the socioeconomic ladder, who have no regard for the poor and lowly. No matter how high they get, however, there are always people who are higher than they, looking down on them. And so they cannot be content till they get to the next rung of the ladder" *(Ecclesiastes: A New Translation with Introduction* [Anchor Bible], 218).

Get used to it. This is the way it will always be. Do not get sucked up into this kind of lifestyle. This is not what God gives us "the land" for. Land is intended to produce a yield, to feed people, not to be hoarded as a means of social status and wealth. "Woe to those who join house to house, who add field to field, until there is no more room, and you are made to dwell alone in the midst of the land" (Isa. 5:8). So, the first point in Solomon's wisdom about wealth is that there will always be someone with more money than you. Learn to live with it.

Solomon's second point (5:10) is that *if you love money you will never have enough*. Human desire always outruns acquisitions, no matter how large the acquisitions may be. It always amazes me how people that are quite wealthy according even to middle-class standards nevertheless complain about not having enough. When I hear someone who makes five to ten times as much as I do complain about being strapped for money, it reminds me of this passage. Likewise, when someone who makes five times less than I do hears me complain about stretching my budget, they are baffled. It's all relative. Money is like seawater; the more a man drinks the more thirsty he becomes. Whether or not you will be content does not have as much to do with how much we have as it often does with how you deal with what you have been given. In and of themselves wealth and labor are unsatisfactory; they bring no ultimate satisfaction, nor do they bring a man or woman leverage or advantage in the world.

This passage is one we Americans need to hear. The problem in our country right now is that our expectations are so heightened that we come to expect more than we can ever hope to acquire. Thus, we constantly live unsatisfied lives.

Solomon's third point supports his second. "When goods increase, they increase who eat them, and what advantage has their owner but to see them with his eyes?" (5:11). One reason wealth does not satisfy is because *the one who increases in wealth increases responsibilities*. These words are written to the man or woman who covets more money. He or she may be poor or rich—both are just as capable of wanting more. "If only I had more money. If only I had this or that, or had this job or that job. It would all be different." As Matthew Henry once observed, "Poor people are as much in danger of an inordinate desire towards the wealth of the world as the rich from an inordinate delight in it." Do you really want more wealth, more "goods," more land and cars and houses and everything else? *Really*? Do you realize that when wealth increases responsibilities increase as well? Do you think you can have one without the other? It is a foolish dream.

Imagine that you suddenly become wealthy. You will now have all kinds of bills and creditors, financial vampires who will be greedy to consume your wealth. Plus, the government will suddenly have an incentive to scrutinize you to get more from you. What good will it be to you? There suddenly appears a swarm of leaches and parasites anxious to benefit from your wealth. And what will you really do with it? Will it really improve your life? Or will you just sit around and look at it?

Solomon moves on to his fourth point. *Increase your wealth and you will experience a corresponding increase in anxiety about the future of that wealth*. "Sweet is the sleep of a laborer, whether he eats little or much, but the full stomach of the rich will not let him sleep" (5:12). The man who lives hand to mouth sleeps easily. He doesn't have much to worry about. He leaves the big issues to his master. But wealth brings sleeplessness and the fear that one simple blunder or oversight may result in the loss of everything. Will you catch the news too late and fail to sell your stocks in time? Have you given your investments over to be managed by a wise man? The evangelical bishop J. C. Ryle said it well: "Money is in truth one of the most unsatisfying of possessions. It takes away some cares, no doubt; but it brings with it quite as many cares as it takes away. There is the trouble in the getting of it. There is anxiety in the keeping of it. There are temptations in the use of it. There is guilt in the abuse of it. There is sorrow in the losing of it. There is perplexity in the disposing of it."

Solomon's fifth point (5:13–14) seems to be that *God has an uncanny way of undermining the security of wealth jealously possessed.* "Do not toil to acquire wealth; be discerning enough to desist. When your eyes light on it, it is gone, for suddenly it sprouts wings, flying like an eagle toward heaven" (Prov. 23:5). Hoarded wealth ruins the man or woman who grasps it so firmly. And wealth can be so vaporous, here one day and gone the next. By some accident or misfortune, the entire estate can be lost. The problem lies in attempting to hoard riches. As Thomas Manton has said, "God gave us wealth, not that we should be hoarders but dispensers."

This "grievous evil" (5:13) through which wealth is lost is nothing other than way in which God providentially curses those who trust in wealth. Solomon has used this expression several times since 1:13: "It is an *unhappy business* that God has given to the children of man to be busy with." There is no way to get around this. You can't spend more money to insure yourself against God's curse.

Tom Wolfe's wonderful book *Bonfire of the Vanities* illustrates Solomon's point rather well. Here was one man—Sherman McCoy—who reached the pinnacle of his profession on Wall Street. He was the king of the bond market making a million dollars a year. He had a place on Park Avenue. He thought of himself as master of the universe. But one wrong turn off the freeway one night led to a series of disasters that brought it all down on his head. God has amazing ways of taking away great wealth. "A faithful man will abound with blessings, but whoever hastens to be rich will not go unpunished" (Prov. 28:20).

If God's curse destroys wealth, then death means this eventually happens to everyone. Solomon's sixth point (5:15) is that *the wealthy man—indeed, every man and woman—must depart the world as naked as he came into the world.* Thus the Puritan Thomas Brooks advised, "It is a very high point of Christian wisdom and prudence always to look upon the good things and the great things of this world as a man will certainly look upon them when he comes to die."

Solomon's seventh point (5:16, 17) is that *despite all this, there will be those who will spend all of their days—days and nights, nights and days—working to amass riches and possessions*. They will consign themselves to lives of frustration, affliction, and anger—to eating "in darkness in much vexation and sickness and anger." They sentence themselves to "toil for the wind." Riches ultimately give men and women no real leverage over the quality of their lives! We look at the people in our culture and we see they are frustrated. They are constantly stressed out. They are afflicted with all sorts of emotional and psychological ailments and they are an angry people who want their fair share of life's goodies. They make themselves into an envious, bitter people. Is that what you want to become?

How much better then, as Solomon finally concludes (5:18–20), to be content with one's "lot" and regard it as "good and fitting" (v. 18). This will keep him from the unhealthy preoccupation with finding the answers and reasons for all of one's troubles (v. 20). Thus we arrive at the same conclusion as before (2:24–26), but which is now deepened and developed to include the confession on the part of the believer that he will accept life as a gift from God and accept his limited place without fretting over trying to pry into God's hidden wisdom. As Old Testament scholar Walter Kaiser explains, "The conclusion (5:18–20) remains the same. Man must get enjoyment, not possessions. And that capacity to enjoy, no matter how great or how small, is a gift from God. It is much better to receive wealth as a gift from God, along with the God-given ability to enjoy it, than to see wealth as an end in itself." The apostle Paul concurs in writing to Timothy:

> Now there is great gain in godliness with contentment, for we brought nothing into the world, and we cannot take anything out of the world. But if we have food and clothing, with these we will be content. But those who desire to be rich fall into temptation, into a snare, into many senseless and harmful desires that plunge people into ruin and destruction. For the love of money is a root of all kinds of evils. It is through this craving that some have wandered away from the faith and pierced themselves with many pangs. But as for you, O man of God, flee these things. Pursue

righteousness, godliness, faith, love, steadfastness, and gentleness. Fight the good fight of the faith. Take hold of the eternal life to which you were called and about which you made the good confession in the presence of many witnesses. (1 Tim. 6:6–12)

Part Three

Ecclesiastes 6:1–8:17

With chapter six, Solomon begins a new cycle in his argument, which, as we now can see more clearly, is that life is to be enjoyed *by faith*. Here Solomon is working toward the conclusion that even though the wicked may prosper, their destiny is certain:

> Though a sinner does evil a hundred times and prolongs his life, yet I know that it will be well with those who fear God, because they fear before him. But it will not be well with the wicked, neither will he prolong his days like a shadow, because he does not fear before God.
>
> There is a [vapor] that takes place on earth, that there are righteous people to whom it happens according to the deeds of the wicked, and there are wicked people to whom it happens according to the deeds of the righteous. I said that this also is [vapor]. And I commend joy, for man has no good thing under the sun but to eat and drink and be joyful, for this will go with him in his toil through the days of his life that God has given him under the sun. (Eccl. 8:12–15)

This is the goal to which Solomon is taking us in this section. He begins by making a startling statement in 6:1–6 (that a man may be better off non-existent) and leads the perceptive reader to begin asking all kinds of questions. This has been Solomon's intention all along. He is taking us deeper and deeper with him on his journey. To accomplish this, he often begins his sections with observations mixed with questions and relative judgments (this is *better* than that), only to end the section with answers and advice. In this case the major questions of this section are powerfully presented in chapter 6, relative judgments are made in chapter 7 and parts of chapter 8, and then the answer is given, once again, in 8:12–14, together with the advice that he has given before at the end of this section in 8:17.

8

Discerning Good, Better, and Best: Ecclesiastes 6:1–7:12

Whoever desires to love life and see good days, let him keep his tongue from evil and his lips from speaking deceit.
—1 Peter 3:10 (Psalm 34:10)

Ask someone if they would want to be a famous movie star and you usually hear an affirmative answer. But what if you asked people if they wanted to be Christopher Reeves, the *Superman* actor who spent years completely paralyzed before finally dying from complications related to his paralysis? Suddenly, having fame and wealth doesn't seem so important. We all know it is no good to have things if you are deprived of the ability to enjoy those things. I remember when I was a child and got fitted for braces. Then and every time thereafter, when I got them tightened, I found myself unable to enjoy food. It was terribly frustrating. I would sit at the family table watching everyone else eat all they wanted while I could do no more than drink chicken broth. I *wanted* the food so much it made me miserable, but I could enjoy none of it. It was maddening.

In the conclusion to the last section, Solomon ascribed all good to God: "Everyone also to whom God has given wealth and possessions and power to enjoy them, and to accept his lot and rejoice in his toil—this is the gift of God" (5:19). Now Solomon admits to a problem in life, that in fact there are those who have been given great things but who have not been given the power to enjoy them.

> There is an evil that I have seen under the sun, and it lies heavy on mankind: a man to whom God gives wealth, possessions, and honor, so that he lacks nothing of all that he desires, yet God does not give him power to enjoy them, but a stranger enjoys them. This is [vapor]; it is a grievous evil. (6:1–2)

Literally, verse two says that God has not made the person able "to eat from them" (NASB). For such a person, Solomon tells us it is exactly like having a full plate of your favorite food set before you when you cannot eat it. When you are sick, of course, you do not care, but when something else prevents you from enjoying such food, it is maddening. The world is like a large table spread before us, which God gives to us to eat, to consume, to enjoy as a gift from God. But to enjoy and to discern the goodness of the gift is the key. Prosperity without the divine gift of enjoyment is nothing. It is vapor, like having braces on your life.

Pay attention to the flow of Solomon's meditation. The problem, the "evil" or "tragedy," is stated in stark terms in the first two verses. Solomon says that there are those among mankind who get all that they desire but are not given the power to enjoy it. Eventually strangers are the ones to enjoy it, while the one who worked for it does not. This is vapor and shepherding the wind. Then in verses three through six, the person who lacks nothing is described twice in extravagant terms:

> If a man fathers a hundred children and lives many years, so that the days of his years are many, but his soul is not satisfied with the good, and he also has no burial, I say that a stillborn child is better off than he. For it comes in [vapor] and goes in darkness, and in darkness its name is covered. Moreover, it has not seen the sun or known anything, yet it finds rest rather than he. Even though he should live a thousand years twice over, yet not see the good—do not all go to the one place? (6:3–6)

Solomon offers two "illustrations" of the person who has everything but cannot enjoy what he has. First, he is described as someone with many children who lives to be a hundred years old (6:3). The vapor of life is described as something worse than being a miscarriage. The man has no control over what happens after he dies, so he cannot guarantee himself a proper burial. If he cannot see satisfaction in the good, then it is all vapor. In verses four and five Solomon waxes poetic in describing the "experience" of one born dead. Finally, in verse six, Solomon gets more extravagant and says it doesn't matter if someone was to live twice two thousand years, they are better off unborn if they "see no good."

We learned at the end of chapter 5 that as a general rule God has given mankind to enjoy what they have (5:19–20). He has given them material possessions and authorized them to partake of what they produce as their portion. This is the manifestation of God's gift to humanity. Yet there are all-too-common instances when the gift is given, but God does not give a person the power to enjoy the wealth, possessions, and honor he has bestowed (6:1–6). This is an aspect of the "work of affliction" that God has laid upon fallen humanity.

Solomon's initial conclusion—that such a person is better off unborn—may startle us, but there is no getting around his plain statement. You are better off not having entered the world rather than being a fruitful parent with a long life who does not experience true satisfaction. Being is not good in itself. Existence is only good if it is experienced in relationship to God and enjoyed according to his good gifts.

Jesus once said that a certain man would have been better off never having existed: "It would have been better for that man if he had not been born" (Matt. 26:24b). One can easily imagine the objections. *Wait a minute. I thought existence in itself was good. I thought that to be or to be born is in itself something good.* Apparently that is not the case, for Solomon says the same thing. For some men it would have been better if they had been miscarried or stillborn.

In the case of Judas, we can understand why Jesus said this, since Jesus knew Judas's destiny. We might think that such a judgment could possibly apply to people who are poor or sick or afflicted with some terrible disease, but we would be wrong to think such a thing. Solomon's wise judgment is pronounced precisely against the man who has riches, honor, numerous children, and a long, healthy life. Such a man would have been better off never having been born *if* that person failed to "be satisfied with the good" (6:3).

In the words of Solomon, one must be given "to see the good" in life. What does this mean? The NIV translators think that Solomon is using "the good" (*tov*) here in a psychological sense, that a man must be able to enjoy his prosperity. I think he is using "the good" in Ecclesiastes in a teleological sense. To *see* the good means to *discern* the point or purpose of it all. Let's see how Solomon unpacks this in the following paragraphs.

Solomon goes on to reiterate the same point poetically and emphasize the problem of human insatiability.

> All the toil of man is for his mouth, yet his appetite is not satisfied. For what advantage has the wise man over the fool? And what does the poor man have who knows how to conduct himself before the living? Better is the sight of the eyes than the wandering of the appetite: this also is [vapor] and [shepherding the wind]. (Eccl. 6:7–9)

Note the language of eating and consumption (also in 6:2) in reference to man's life and work. It is better to discern the good in your present life than to die on account of your insatiability (6:9).

Finally, Solomon returns to the point he made in verse two that "God does not give him the power to eat of it."

> Whatever has come to be has already been named, and it is known what man is, and that he is not able to dispute with one stronger than he. The more words, the more [vapor], and what is the advantage to man? For who knows what is good for man while he lives the few days of his [vaporous] life, which he passes like a shadow? For who can tell man what will be after him under the sun? (Eccl. 6:10–12)

Solomon is reminding us that it is God who has ordained this state of affairs. It is the result of his curse, the burden he has laid upon men, as we saw back in 1:13. According to the ordinance of God, the creation cannot yield ultimate enjoyment without the fear of God. Not one of us has the power to challenge God's determination of our lives. He is the one who knows what we are and who is stronger than we are. You can wrestle and contest God's curse, but you will fail in it. God has determined to frustrate man by means of the material creation.

"The more words, the more vapor, and what is the advantage to man?" You can talk about it all you want. You can write about it all you want. This will not relieve the situation, but compound the vaporous, uncontrollable quality of your life. The true path of wisdom is for a man to acknowledge his limitations—his complicity in the rebellion that has brought about God's curse in the first place—and begin to fear God. Who knows what is really good for us? God knows. That is the answer that Solomon continues to return to at the conclusion of each wave of his investigation. Here in verse twelve we find something that sounds like the apostle Paul defending God's righteousness in Romans 9:20, saying, "Who are you, O man, to answer back to God?" Prosperity is not always what it seems; therefore, we should seek to know and fear God and be content with such gifts as he gives us, and to ask for and receive the gift of enjoyment from his hands.

One cannot fail to note the challenge here to the American way of life, especially the notion that a long life is a good life and a wealthy man or woman is a satisfied man or woman. What good is your life? What is the purpose of your life? Toward what is it oriented? What is the point? These are the real questions. And Solomon is headed toward a real answer, though it requires faith: "Though a sinner does evil a hundred times and prolongs his life, yet I know that it will be well with those who fear God, because they fear before him" (Eccl. 8:12). So what is the point of prolonging life if your life has no transcendent orientation, no relationship to the Creator of that life? If you have not "seen the good," if your soul is not satisfied with the good (6:3), then what is the use of a long life? The fundamental problem is that people are not given to see the purpose of what they have been given. They are not able to find satisfaction in work, possessions, or a long, healthy life that they have worked so hard to achieve by dieting and exercise.

We should note here the probing point. *Wealth is not automatically a sign of blessing from God*! One cannot extrapolate from the possession of wealth to the assurance that God blesses the wealthy one. This is a key insight into the wisdom literature of Israel. The kings of Israel have matured and can now discern that material blessing often comes at a price. "Never judge a book by its cover" goes the saying. Similarly, we should never confuse the true state of another person's life by looking merely at the outward welfare. A man or woman may possess wealth, possessions, honor, numerous children, and health all throughout life and yet he or she may be a miserable person who has failed to discern life's true purpose and therefore life's true joys.

The materialistic, unbelieving German philosopher Ludwig von Feuerbach was the one who said "Man is what he eats." He thought he was vanquishing Christianity with that maxim, but as the late brilliant Eastern Orthodox theologian Alexander Schmemman has noted, he was in fact, without knowing it, expressing a biblical fact about man. In the biblical story of creation, man is presented first of all as a hungry being, and the whole world is given to him to consume. Man must eat to live. He must take the world into his body and transform it into himself. Schmemman says:

> He is indeed what he eats, and the whole world is presented as one all-embracing banquet table for man. And this image of the banquet remains, throughout the whole Bible, the central image of life. It is the image of life at its creation, and also the image of life at its end and fulfillment: ". . . that you eat and drink at my table in my Kingdom." (*For the Life of the World* [New York: St. Vladimir's Seminary Press, 1973], 11)

The sin of man is that he ceased to be hungry for God. We have ceased to see our whole lives, everything we consume, as a sacrament of communion with God. The sin of all sins, the truly original sin, is not a transgression of mere rules, but first of all, the deviation of man's love and desire from their proper object, the Lord God himself. That man prefers something else to God—the world, possessions, children, life, health—this is the real sin. The Lord himself is our highest good. All other goods are only good in relation to him. This is one of Saint Augustine's great contributions to spirituality: *use* and *enjoy* the things of this world but *love* God alone. Only when we love God are we able to properly use and enjoy the gifts God gives us in this world.

The problem of happiness (or satisfaction) is this: to know whom one should desire in order to be happy, and to know how to obtain him. The wise man discovers that he cannot be the source of his own enjoyment; he must discover in his humility his utter dependence upon God for life and satisfaction. And so Jesus truly is wisdom from God (1 Cor. 1:30), for he is the way, the truth, and the life (John 14:6). "The thief comes only to steal and kill and destroy. I came that they may have life and have it abundantly" (John 10:10).

GOOD, BETTER, BEST

It is a common occurrence in the life of an adult dealing with small children. A child may run to her parents' bed because she is scared of a nightmare, and Christian parents will often assure their little one that she shouldn't worry because God will protect her. When teaching on honesty we simply tell our young children that lying is always wrong, but we know that God does not always keep us from harm, even horrible tragedy, and we know that saying something contrary to fact is sometimes mandatory (Jas. 2:25). Nevertheless, what we tell our young children is good and right. They aren't supposed to handle the complexity of life until later. We need to give them black and white answers and instructions. They start simple, but they are not supposed to stay that way. Israel was given the Law in her infancy, but later she was given wisdom because it was time for her to admit and deal with the complexity of life.

Almost every problem I am confronted with as a pastor—a problem where I am asked or expected to give biblical advice—does not lend itself to a black and white answer. It requires wisdom, wisdom that I am too often lacking. *Pastor, what should I do?* Some people are looking for a magic verse that will give them some supernatural answer. Others hope that there is a *law* that will make their decision easy. It almost never happens that way. Sometimes, it does. Obviously, when God commands, we must obey! More often than not, however, the advice must be given in terms of *good*, *better*, and *best*, or *bad*, *worse*, and *worst*. That kind of advice requires careful analysis by the person involved, careful inquiry into his or her motives, into the complexity of one's situation, and spiritual attentiveness to the Word of God. Living as Christians requires *wisdom*.

Biblical wisdom is a function of character and experience. It involves know-how. It entails skill, observation, contemplation, experience, and discernment. These are qualities that cannot be bought or memorized. They are capabilities that must be developed over time. One such quality or capability that must be cultivated by us is that of learning to make what I will call *comparative judgments*. Listen to how Solomon puts it in 7:1–12:

> A good name is better than precious ointment,
>   and the day of death than the day of birth.
> It is better to go to the house of mourning
>   than to go to the house of feasting,
> for this is the end of all mankind,
>   and the living will lay it to heart.

> Sorrow is better than laughter,
> for by sadness of face the heart is made glad.
> The heart of the wise is in the house of mourning,
> but the heart of fools is in the house of mirth.
> It is better for a man to hear the rebuke of the wise
> than to hear the song of fools.
> For as the crackling of thorns under a pot,
> so is the laughter of the fools;
> this also is [vapor].
> Surely oppression drives the wise into madness,
> and a bribe corrupts the heart.
> Better is the end of a thing than its beginning,
> and the patient in spirit is better than the proud in spirit.
> Be not quick in your spirit to become angry,
> for anger lodges in the bosom of fools.
> Say not, "Why were the former days better than these?"
> For it is not from wisdom that you ask this.
> Wisdom is good with an inheritance,
> an advantage to those who see the sun.
> For the protection of wisdom is like the protection of money,
> and the advantage of knowledge is that
> wisdom preserves the life of him who has it.

Chapter 7 is a special challenge to interpreters because Solomon changes his style. Now he gives us *proverbs*. Instead of reflections and arguments he writes pithy maxims that hold deeper truths, but Solomon's change in style is not the only problem. We must all confess, if we are honest with ourselves, that we have some difficulty navigating the book of Ecclesiastes. We are not at home in the wisdom books of the Hebrew Scriptures. We are more comfortable with laws or commands: "Do this" and "Do not do that." They give us black and white absolute judgments about right and wrong, but that is not what wisdom literature offers us.

We like things cut and dried. I suspect this has to do partly with the cultural baggage that we have inherited. Maybe it is also evidence of our immaturity as a Christian culture. We resist mature wisdom. We are often quite content to remain spiritual children.

Solomon has just posed the question to us at the end of chapter 6: "For who knows what is good for man while he lives the few days of his vain life, which he passes like a shadow?" (Eccl. 6:12). The *provisional* answer offered by Solomon in chapter 7 comes as a series of seven *relative* goods. The mature man or woman will learn to be wise by valuing what is *better* in life by making useful comparative judgments.

It may appear at first glance that all of these comparative evaluations are free-floating and loosely attached. That is a common first impression, but readers should be careful; that is only a superficial judgment. Proverbial assessments normally have this deeper, riddle-like character. Solomon's various play on words and his sophisticated way of linking all of this material together with repetitions of vocabulary and themes make it certain that there is some deeper unity to this passage. These sayings are not haphazardly thrown together, but they are not meant to be understood easily, either. Remember Solomon's programmatic statement about wisdom writing in the first chapter of Proverbs.

> The proverbs of Solomon, son of David, king of Israel:
>
> To know wisdom and instruction,
> to understand words of insight,
> to receive instruction in wise dealing,
> in righteousness, justice, and equity;
> to give prudence to the simple,
> knowledge and discretion to the youth—
> Let the wise hear and increase in learning,
> and the one who understands obtain guidance,
> *to understand a proverb and a saying,*
> the words of the wise *and their riddles.*
>
> The fear of the LORD is the beginning of knowledge;
> fools despise wisdom and instruction. (Prov. 1:1–7; emphasis added)

Solomon is telling us that his words must be figured out. They are riddles that, in the process of wrestling with them, will grant us wisdom. "It is the glory of God to conceal things, but the glory of kings is to search things out" (Prov. 25:2). What do we learn by searching out these proverbs?

Once again, the backdrop to all of these comparative judgments is the experience of suffering and affliction or oppression—the heavy burden that God has laid upon the sons of Adam (1:13). Solomon has learned to be honest about our life under the sun. This is a challenge to us. How does the wise man or woman respond to such burdens, to such afflictions and evils? What is good, better, and best?

We want life to be trouble-free and entirely enjoyable, to be devoid of risk and suffering and death. We cover reality with smiley faces and shallow clichés. We talk about thinking positively or thinking good thoughts and everything will just be fine. This is, at best, immaturity. If we refuse to grow up to a better view, then it is more than immaturity; it is foolishness. Do you want to be a wise man or woman? You want to know what's good for a man or woman in this life? Then you should make these comparative judgments in your life.

We have here six sayings that prominently feature the Hebrew word for good (*tov*). They naturally group into doubles and can be outlined this way:

1. Death is a better instructor of the living than birth (7:1–4).
2. Rebuke is better than frivolous praise (7:5–7).
3. Patient hope is better than arrogant whining (7:8–10).

This section is capped off with a seventh *tov* saying (7:11–12) regarding the relative advantage of wisdom.

First, *death is a better instructor of the living than birth* (7:1–4). While we all probably understand (whether we remember to practice it or not) that a good name is better than precious ointment, we have a lot harder time figuring out why the day of death is better than the day we were born. Solomon is *not* saying that death is desirable because life is meaningless. Nor is Solomon arguing that death is preferable to life, or that to choose death is wise. He is not an advocate for the Hemlock Society. Solomon is not making a *general* statement saying that death is good and life is bad. After all, precious ointment is not bad. If precious ointment were really worthless then a good name would not be all that valuable. The point of a relative judgment is that one is good, even great, but that something else is better. The day of one's birth is a good and precious thing in Solomon's statement.

Then how is the day of one's death better than the day one is born? Solomon, remember, is interested in how and when one acquires true, godly wisdom (6:11–12). From one angle, this is almost common sense. Maturity takes time. Wisdom comes with experience (if experienced rightly). Obviously, one must grow older (toward the day of one's death) in order to grow wiser.

Solomon elaborates (7:2) that the "house of mourning" (i.e., a funeral) is preferable to feasting. This gives us a further interpretive clue as to how the day of death is preferable to the day of birth. The person who has died is not one of the mourners at his or her own funeral. No, it is the *living* that mourn the death of someone. Solomon does not mean that it is better to go to the house of mourning in a pine box, but as a visitor drawn into the circle of the bereaved. So, also, in verse one, it is probably not your *own* day of death that is better than the day of birth. Rather, it is that you have more of an opportunity to learn true wisdom at the passing of a loved one than you do at the birth of a child. Death "is the end of all mankind and the living will lay it to heart" (7:2b). The wise man can learn from participating in the wake of another's death.

The living should ponder the inescapable end of every person—death. Consider what this means for your living. Come to terms with this. Do not ignore it. Do not act as if you are not going to die. Do not continue to put off dealing with the implications.

In God's providence, I studied Ecclesiastes at a point when I had begun thinking of death often. Perhaps it was turning forty that started this trend, or thinking of my youngest child's life and my eventual absence from it. I think it comes with age. Young people are able to put death out of their minds. For this reason, they do not always act wisely. Wisdom comes with age, because age brings you closer to death, and death occasions serious reflection upon the meaning of one's life. Solomon is telling us that is what *should* happen when one grows older. The fool thinks of only his own titillation and so detaches his mind from associations with death.

The day of death is better because it has more to teach us. At birth or indeed at any time of transition (graduation, birthdays, promotions), the mood is excited and expansive. We don't dwell on human mortality or weakness. We don't say to the person next to us at a baptism, "He's going to die someday, you know." In fact, just the opposite: we speculate about the newborn's future fame and glory. Our hopes and dreams run free. That is not the case on the day of death, at the house of mourning. Then, the mood is thoughtful and contemplative. The fact of human mortality is plain. You can ignore it and refuse to deal with it; but the death of a friend or relative is the best time to face the grim reality. Every funeral anticipates our own.

This indicates that we should be wise about Christian funerals. It is true that we do not grieve as those without the hope of the gospel. Nevertheless, there is nothing beneficial about turning a funeral into a birthday party. If Jesus wept at Lazarus's grave when he was going to bring him back to life in a moment, how much more should we mourn those we lose for the rest of our lives? Christians may mean well and have a pious rationale when they put on their "happy faces" at a funeral, but what they are doing may indicate that they are afraid to face facts and reflect upon the curse that is so powerful everywhere under the sun.

Funerals are not the only place we find a false view of Christian piety that denies Solomon's wisdom. For example, it is *not* the proper function of Christian devotional booklets to help you to think positively about the upcoming day. Unfortunately, with the rise of the cult of positive thinking, many Christian devotionals surgically remove all of the happy, uplifting passages in the Bible and assemble them in lovely little noncontextual collections. I wonder if you can find Ecclesiastes 7:1–4 in any of the popular monthly Christian devotionals.

It is *right* for us to grieve and cry and mourn! Sorrow and sadness are appropriate as a response to death. Refusal to think about death is a proof of one's folly; it is never pious. "Sorrow is better than laughter," not because it is better to be sad all the time but because sadness can lead to wisdom and thus to better joy—"by sadness the face of the heart is made glad" (7:3). Solomon is not equating sadness and sorrow with wisdom, as if the wise man will never wear a smile or enjoy himself. The truly wise person will appreciate the value of a crisis, and not seek to anesthetize himself to these times by engaging in frivolous, distracting pleasures. You must make the proper appraisal of the opportunities afforded by birth and death. Ecclesiastes is following here the wisdom of Moses found in Psalm 90, the psalm of human mortality: "So teach us to number our days that we may get a heart of wisdom."

The wise man must ponder the significance of death. If you are to be wise, then you must not ignore death, you must rather devote your mind to understanding what it means for living. The fool seeks distractions.

There is another relative judgment that the Christian will make in order to acquire wisdom. *The Christian will judge rebuke as better than frivolous praise* (7:5–6): "It is better for a man to hear the rebuke of the wise than to hear the song of fools. For as the crackling of thorns under a pot, so is the laughter of fools; this is also [vapor]." Many centuries ago, Augustine showed he had learned the wisdom of Solomon by writing, "Far rather would I be censured by anyone whatsoever, than be praised by either the erring or the flatterer. For the lover of truth need fear no one's censure. For he that censures, must needs be either enemy of friend. And if an enemy reviles, he must be borne with: but a friend, if he errs, must be taught; if he teaches, listened to" (*On the Trinity*, 1.3.5).

Thorns aren't usually used as kindling to generate heat. A bramble bush has slender stalks that produce barely enough heat to warm a pot, but in the process the burning thorns generate a lot of noise—crackling and popping that is irrelevant to the task of cooking. This is like the fool's laughter. It is useless. Like the noise of sticks burning, praise or flattery from a fool has no instructional value. His word is like unfiltered noise that has not passed through the filter of a trained mind. The truest form of joy, the most lasting, is the one that is not escapist or anesthetizing, but fully informed. We should desire not the "song" (7:5) or the "laughter" (7:6) of fools, but "the rebuke of the wise" (7:5).

> Let a righteous man strike me—it is a kindness;
> let him rebuke me—it is oil for my head;
> let my head not refuse it.
> Yet my prayer is continually against their evil deeds. (Ps. 141:5)

Again, Solomon is not in love with pain. He thinks rebukes are good because of where they lead us. "For the moment all discipline seems painful rather than pleasant, but later it yields the peaceful fruit of righteousness to those who have been trained by it" (Heb. 12:11). Of course, the problem is that many times we are too impatient to reach the peaceful fruit of righteousness. Especially in times of personal suffering we tend to want to hear the flattery of fools. Thus Solomon warns that affliction (v. 7; not "oppression" as some translate it, but all trials) can drive even the wise to accept the songs of a fool. Such comforting drivel constitutes a bribe (v. 7).

Much of the sobering instruction that a wise man ought to heed is constantly set over against the foolish whitewashing of suffering with frivolous escapist entertainment. There will always be foolish people who prefer to laugh and sing and feast rather than reflect upon death and sorrow and oppression. Solomon's point is that such a life is seductively attractive. Jesus later referred to it as "the *deceitfulness* of riches" (Matt. 13:22).

Finally, *patient hope is better than arrogant whining* (7:8–10). One way to refuse to face facts is to pretend that the problems of life are not inherent in life under the sun or due to God's action in laying a heavy burden on man. Rather, they are of recent making. People embrace whining instead of wisdom. Solomon now warns us against what the Roman poet Horace called *laudator temporis acti* ("a praiser of the past"). This happened in the later years of the Roman Empire, when everyone whined about "the good old days of the Republic." True wisdom does not champion the past over the present. This is a problem with much of "conservatism."

A nostalgic escape into the past is foolish. The man or woman who wants to resurrect what is dead and gone gives evidence of a desire for easy answers, and such a desire could easily lead to anger over things that cannot be helped or changed (7:8–9). Anger is often associated with such foolish longing. Many will excuse it as righteous anger, but it does not accomplish anything (Jas. 1:20). The wise man does not idealize the past. It is foolish to dwell upon the past as the ideal from which we have declined. A wise person will never even ask such a question. From wisdom's point of view, the question holds no meaning.

The conclusion of the matter comes in 7:11–12. Now that Solomon has shown us how the wise person approaches life—how the wise Christian's mind and life are formed and how the fool's mind is distracted—we can appreciate the next better-than saying, the last exercise in comparative discernment.

Solomon had asked, "Who knows what is good?" (6:12). Now he tells us unambiguously: wisdom is good! An inheritance (7:11) is something expected at a future date, either shortly before or upon the death of one's father. So also wisdom's benefits are not always realized immediately. One must be patient. If one has made the six wise comparative evaluations that Solomon has enumerated in the first eleven verses, then one can hope for the benefits of that wisdom in the future.

The high point of this section is Solomon's connecting *yithrown* (advantage, leverage) with wisdom, and defining it as that which gives life (7:12). There is no advantage in labor alone. Advantage in life is available to the wise alone. Such wisdom and knowledge are a shelter to the wise man, the guarantee of the preservation of his life in all of its fullness.

Wisdom, remember, is a path one can choose, a way one can go. The alternative is the way of folly. Here Solomon has spelled out the way of wisdom.

What path are you on?

9

A Riddle Wrapped in a Mystery Inside an Enigma: Ecclesiastes 7:13–8:17

For as the heavens are higher than the earth, so are my ways higher than your ways and my thoughts than your thoughts. —Isaiah 55:9

There is a pervasive brand of Christianity out there that deserves the title "foolishness." Ministers, churches, and so-called Christian movements teach in such a way as to produce nothing less than *fools*. It goes by many names: "Faith Promise," "Word Faith," or "Seed Faith," to name a few. It may not use these designations. It may just be thought of as *relevant*, helpful, and attractive "applied" Christianity. Thousands of books and pamphlets line the bookshelves of Christian bookstores with titles like *How to Write Your Own Ticket With God*, *Godliness is Profitable*, *The Laws of Prosperity*, *God's Creative Power Will Work for You*, *God's Formula for Success and Prosperity*, *God's Master Key to Prosperity*, or even *How to Raise Godly*

Children. And don't forget several that boil down to *Dieting God's Way*. The basic idea (or principle or law) is that your behavior, your prayers, and your righteous living or giving can insure from God a long life, prosperity, and whatever else you want. There is no mystery in God's way with us. Rather, his procedures are transparent and if you learn them, you can write your own ticket in life.

It may be easy to point our fingers and say, "Ha! This is silly." But the truth is that within our own depraved breast we all have the tendency to think that God is at our beck and call—that whatever else happens to others, our faith, our good works, and our righteous life will insure God's uninterrupted blessing in our lives. In fact, this is a particular temptation to suburban congregations of middle-class people. We attract people by telling them that we know how God works and that God can do wonders for their lives. More than likely, churches are planted in our own denominations with this kind of preaching. There is an emphasis on "relevant" practical sermons about how to do this and how to do that. If you just follow these principles, the congregation is told, you can find happiness and success in business. You can insure security in your family finances. By following these rules in disciplining your children you can even manage the final product. You should raise kids God's way because everyone else is raising theirs Satan's way.

This is, strictly speaking, *foolish*. It is not wise. True wisdom recognizes God's unmanageable disposition over your earthly life. True wisdom consists in fearing God. The person who thinks he can gain leverage reveals a heart of unbelief. "He has an unhealthy craving for controversy and for quarrels about words, which produce envy, dissension, slander, evil suspicions, and constant friction among people who are depraved in mind and deprived of the truth, *imagining that godliness is a means of gain*" (1 Tim. 6:4–5; emphasis added). James addresses the issue of what true religious wisdom should look like from another angle:

> Come now, you who say, "Today or tomorrow we will go into such and such a town and spend a year there and trade and make a profit"—yet you do not know what tomorrow will bring. What

> is your life? For you are a mist that appears for a little time and then vanishes. Instead you ought to say, "If the Lord wills, we will live and do this or that." As it is, you boast in your arrogance. All such boasting is evil. (4:13–16)

True Christian wisdom "sees" how God works in this fallen world and the wise believer confesses that God does what he does and nothing we can do binds him. We don't control the future and we don't have a means of gain, even in godliness. This is genuine wisdom—wisdom that *fears* God. Do you think you are wise? Then ask yourself if you fear God.

God is to be feared because the living and true God controls your life and destiny; indeed, he is the ultimate origin of everything that happens to you—whether good or bad.

> Consider the work of God:
> who can make straight what he has made crooked?
>
> In the day of prosperity be joyful, and in the day of adversity consider: God has made the one as well as the other, so that man may not find out anything that will be after him.
>
> In my [vaporous] life I have seen everything. There is a righteous man who perishes in his righteousness, and there is a wicked man who prolongs his life in his evildoing. Be not overly righteous, and do not make yourself too wise. Why should you destroy yourself? Be not overly wicked, neither be a fool. Why should you die before your time? It is good that you should take hold of this, and from that withhold not your hand, for the one who fears God shall come out from both of them. (7:13–18)

Solomon admonishes us especially to meditate on God's control over every detail of our lives during times of calamity and suffering and distress. He tells us to "consider" what God does (7:13). The Hebrew word is "see," which here means evaluate, discern, and come to the proper conclusions. It's easy to attribute one's good times to God; unbelievers do it all the time. The true test of faith is found in how you understand the times of trouble and disaster (7:14). Will you recognize their origin in God's will even if this means confessing that God's ways are inexorably enigmatic to you?

This lesson is also taught in another book, the book of Job (another instance of Biblical wisdom literature). Job is famous for his sufferings and his faith. The important point to note, however, is that God is the instigator and cause of Job's loss and pain. It was God who called Satan's attention to Job (Job 1:8). Job responds in faith by doing exactly what Solomon recommends. Job confesses that in both blessing and suffering, "God has made the one as well as the other" (Eccl. 7:14) by saying, "Naked I came from my mother's womb, and naked shall I return. The Lord gave, and the Lord has taken away; blessed be the name of the Lord." (Job 1:21). Just to make sure we don't miss the point that Job is correct about who is responsible for his horrible circumstances, it is recorded for us that God himself told Satan, "You incited me against him to destroy him without reason" (Job 2:3). In reply, Satan challenges God to "stretch out [his] hand" to torment Job even further (Job 2:5). Since God responds by giving Satan permission to do this, it is clear that Satan himself is one of God's "hands."

Job responds to this further torment by confessing that both good and evil come from God and we should accept one as well as the other—"Shall we receive good from God, and shall we not receive evil?" (Job 2:9–10). God's meeting with Job eventually "resolves" the story. God simply questions Job as to his own knowledge and control in comparison to God's. In the process, it becomes clear again that even Satan (as Leviathan) is under God's control (38–40). Job is overwhelmed and confesses his limitations. That is the only answer that the story gives us! There can be no further answer because the entire point is that man cannot understand why God runs the universe the way he does. We must *trust* him.

Your future is hidden in God's secret will. It is unavailable to you. "In the day of prosperity be joyful, and in the day of adversity consider: God has made the one as well as the other, *so that man may not find out anything that will be after him*" (Eccl. 7:14; emphasis added). God answers to no one but himself. He shares his power with no one. He has not relinquished his control to the forces of nature or the randomness of chance or the whimsical nature of the human will.

The Christian who genuinely fears God will repudiate any attempt to manipulate God's disposition of his future. God frustrates our attempts to discover what he does, specifically when we predict what he will do (7:14c). Solomon points out that his life is "vaporous" (7:15a). It is *hebel*. It is not only unpredictable, but *unmanageable*. Remember that "meaningless life" is an inaccurate translation. Solomon's life was not meaningless or empty, and neither is yours. Rather it was *vapor*—unpredictable and uncontrollable, ungovernable and unmanageable. His life was like a mist, just as our lives are. It produced more questions than answers and was beyond his control.

As you read this section, you need to remember what Solomon wrote near the beginning of Ecclesiastes: "What is crooked cannot be made straight, and what is lacking cannot be counted" (Eccl. 1:15). The wise man carefully evaluates the implications of what he "sees" (cf. 14a). What does he see? "There is a righteous man who perishes in his righteousness, and there is a wicked man who prolongs his life in his evildoing." (7:15).

Since evangelicals have used Paul's quotation of Psalm 14:1–3 (found in Romans 3:10) non-contextually to deny that there are any persons who are righteous, I should point out that the Hebrew uses two participles to assure us that the two kinds of men here display good and evil lifestyles—continuous patterns of living—rather than occasional good and evil acts. This is a perfectly valid way for Christians to speak. The apostle John writes in the same way saying, "And now, little children, abide in him [Jesus], so that when he appears we may have confidence and not shrink from him in shame at his coming. If you know that he is righteous, you may be sure that everyone who practices righteousness has been born of him" (1 John 2:28–29). John is following the inspired example of the psalms, which often speak of "the righteous" over against "the wicked."

Nevertheless, properly identifying a man or woman as "righteous" is one thing, however, making assumptions about what that means for the "quality" of their everyday life (or death) is something else entirely. The righteous, like the wicked, sometimes experience an early and untimely death. In American pop theology a long life is supposedly a reward for good behavior. However, Solomon tells us the truth—a truth we will all acknowledge if we consider what we see around us every day. These two lifestyles, righteousness and wickedness, are linked with fates that seem incongruous. Our televangelism takes the position of Job's three "friends" who made false accusations against him. What did they say? "Remember: who that was innocent ever perished? Or where were the upright cut off? As I have seen, those who plow iniquity and sow trouble reap the same" (Job 4:7–8). Job, they argued, must not be righteous or else God would grant him a better life now. This is childish, immature, and ultimately *foolish* theology.

Solomon says that, according to his observations, this happens sufficiently often enough to remind us that these matters cannot be explained by reference to some law or principle. You cannot guarantee anything by your behavior. Now comes the mandate, the wise advice from Solomon that follows upon his observation of the unpredictability of one's future. The connection between 7:3–15 and 7:16–17 *must* be understood or you will go dangerously wrong in applying these two commands to your life. Specifically, our righteous behavior does not call forth anything like a reward from God. The two imperatives (7:16–17) offer two possible responses to the situation described in verse fifteen. The "righteousness" that one is warned against is pursuing piety to elicit a reward. "Be not overly righteous, and do not make yourself too wise" (7:16). As one commentator puts it, this is "an overstrained righteousness which grows out of conceit and stands ready to challenge God for his failure to reward."

Solomon also teaches that the Christian who genuinely fears God will not therefore foolishly think that *his manner of living does not matter*, only that it does not bind God to reward him with life or health or any other good thing in this life. "Be not overly wicked, neither be a fool. Why should you die before your time?" (7:17). These two verses are not symmetrical. We know that God does indeed punish wickedness in this life. It is more likely that you will die from a direct pursuit of wickedness than that you will live a long life because of your righteousness.

Solomon's conclusion anticipates his final admonition at the end of this third movement in his overall argument (8:15). "It is good to grasp the one and not let go of the other. The man who fears God will come forth from them both" (7:18). We must not be misled into false options here. Some *think* that this is cynicism—that Solomon shuts out any gleam of faith here and speaks as an unbeliever. They think that Solomon is actually advocating half-heartedness in the matter of good and evil, because it does not get you anywhere anyway. Some think that verse eighteen advocates a healthy mixture of both good and evil, as if a person may as well enjoy the best of both lifestyles. Such a reading is quite superficial. We must keep this verse together with the whole context (7:15–18). Solomon's wisdom is that we must be careful to avoid false righteousness and also shun evil behavior; but not just to prolong your life, but *out of the fear of God*. The man who fears God will come forth from them both. That is, he will shun false righteousness as well as evil.

God cannot be manipulated by our behavior. He is not to be coddled or possessed or used. He is to be feared. Solomon presents wisdom as fearing God (compare Proverbs 1:7). God is not safe. He is not manageable. His ways are not your ways, his thoughts not your thoughts. He does not follow your rationalizations.

In the Bible, those "who fear the Lord" are identified as God's people. The fear of God is crucially important to living before him (Ps. 33:18; 36:1; Prov. 3:7; Rom. 3:18; Rev. 19:5). Notice that these texts are found in both testaments.

It is important to realize that fear means fear. Even though it is reverential fear and even though you also love and trust God, you may not evacuate the word "fear" of the element of terror, trepidation, alarm, or dread. You cannot collapse fear into faith or love. Fear is a crucial element of the believer's personal response to the living God. Because we trust God's Word, we know that he is a God to be feared.

Subtract fear from a Christian's response to God and what remains is a faithless Christian. Jesus, the full revelation of God himself, evoked fear in his closest disciples, especially when they were treated to a brief manifestation of his absolute dominion over creation. When Jesus stood up and, with a mere word, calmed the storm, "they were filled with great fear and said to one another, 'Who then is this, that even wind and sea obey him?' " (Mark 4:41).

Do you fear God? In a sense, Ecclesiastes is written to help you do so. Just think about how much you know of God's plan for your life and how much control you have over the future, but there is more that you do not know. Not only are God and his ways mysterious, but fallen human nature is also inscrutable.

THE MYSTERY OF FALLEN HUMAN NATURE

What would happen to you if you were forced to fix your own car when it broke down or needed maintenance? How long would you be driving the same vehicle? Would you have to buy a new one every couple of years? Perhaps you are competent enough with cars you could take care of yours if you had the time. Perhaps you feel confident enough to be sure you could teach yourself what to do. Personally, cars baffle me, and I am sure that for some people, there is no question that the automobile engine is a riddle that they will never ever solve.

In various areas of life we all know that there are things that are a complete mystery to us. For some of us it might be foreign languages. For others it might be lawn care. For some of us, it is computers that we can never really figure out. We may be able to operate one that works well, but as soon as something goes wrong we are incapable of searching out the solution. In such cases, we rely on others who know about those things. We think of them as knowledgeable or "wise" in their area of expertise, and because of this we could easily associate wisdom with know-how.

Solomon has told us about how we can learn wisdom better from learning our limitations than we can from our days of joy. The day of death is better than the day of birth for gaining true wisdom. He has also pointed out that pursuing wisdom or righteousness for the sake of leverage with God is foolish. Now he extols wisdom but, at the same time, tells us that there is a riddle in life for which *no one* can search out a solution. Wisdom lies not in our ability to do or to figure out, but in recognizing that some riddles will never be solved.

In this case the riddle is human nature, especially fallen human nature. Not only are God's ways beyond our comprehension, but so are our own. This section is held together by the theme of Solomon's search to figure out the human person. Ultimately, wisdom consists in the conviction that sinful man and woman cannot be adequately searched out; that is, a person's life and thoughts and actions cannot be neatly categorized and explained. Fallen men and women, you and I, remain inscrutable—vapor. There are mechanics for cars and "geeks" for computers, but there is no expert on human nature. Human behavior is inscrutable.

> Wisdom gives strength to the wise man more than ten rulers who are in a city.
>
> Surely there is not a righteous man on earth who does good and never sins.
>
> Do not take to heart all the things that people say, lest you hear your servant cursing you. Your heart knows that many times you have yourself cursed others.
>
> All this I have tested by wisdom. I said, "I will be wise," but it was far from me. That which has been is far off, and deep, very deep; who can find it out?
>
> I turned my heart to know and to search out and to seek wisdom and the scheme of things, and to know the wickedness of folly and the foolishness that is madness. And I find something more bitter than death: the woman whose heart is snares and nets, and whose hands are fetters. He who pleases God escapes her, but the sinner is taken by her. Behold, this is what I found, says the Preacher, while adding one thing to another to find the scheme of things—which my soul has sought repeatedly, but I have not found. One man among a thousand I found, but a woman among all these I have not found. See, this alone I found, that God made man upright, but they have sought out many schemes.
>
> Who is like the wise?
> And who knows the interpretation of a thing?

> A man's wisdom makes his face shine,
> and the hardness of his face is changed. (Eccl. 7:19–8:1)

Throughout chapter 7, Solomon repeatedly writes of what can or cannot be *found out*. He focuses on the idea in this chapter (7:14, 24, 26, 27, 28, 29), though it also comes up elsewhere. For example, "He has made everything beautiful in its time. Also, he has put eternity into man's heart, yet so that *he cannot find out* what God has done from the beginning to the end" (Eccl. 3:11). And again, "Then I saw all the work of God, that *man cannot find out* the work that is done under the sun. However much man may toil in seeking, *he will not find it out*. Even though a wise man claims to know, *he cannot find it out*" (8:17). Paradoxically, we will find that wisdom finds out the most important truth by finding out it *cannot find out* much about fallen human nature.

Solomon begins this passage with two sayings coupled with a warning (7:19–22). Verse nineteen functions as a section heading. The wise man knows man and that makes him strong. This whole section deals with the wise man's discerning knowledge of the depravity of man. In fact, the wise man searches out and seeks to understand "the wickedness of folly and the foolishness that is madness" (7:25).

Why does Solomon want to think about such things? Because like Solomon, the wise person knows the depravity of man—both his own and others—and learns to live in terms of it. *That* is the sort of know-how that wisdom brings: the ability to live in a world of sinners, but *living* in such a world is not the same as being able to *explain* or *comprehend* sinful human nature. A quest for *that* sort of pseudo-wisdom will only make life unlivable. Anyone who desires to rule (which means *serve* in the Bible) will need to take this to heart: "Wisdom gives strength to the wise man more than ten rulers who are in a city" (7:19). A father, mother, employer, or teacher who has learned what Solomon is about to describe has more strength than ten foolish rulers in a city.

The first mystery of human nature Solomon deals with is the fact that even those known as righteous will sin. "Surely there is not a righteous man on earth who does good and never sins" (7:20). We must be careful here. This does not mean that there is nobody that can bear the name "righteous" (see 7:15). Rather, even those who are rightly called righteous are not without moral faults. The imperfect verb conveys the sense of constancy or regularity. On some occasions even a righteous man will fail. While wisdom has its advantages, we cannot afford to forget that there are limitations on all men and women. No one is perfectly wise. All sin.

Solomon reminds us that if we aspire to be a wise man or woman, we must not pay too much attention to the criticisms of others: "Do not take to heart all the things people say" (7:21a). You've done the same thing. "Your heart knows that many times you have yourself cursed others" (7:21b). It is easy to judge someone else. It is much more difficult to take responsibility. Solomon is warning about investigating such matters too closely. This is especially true when we hear someone who is "under" us complaining about us. There is no need to press for judgment against every sinful word uttered by our subordinates.

In the church, not only is this a challenge to pastors, but it also applies to many Christians in a local congregation. Any time you volunteer to do anything you may hear complaints. No good deed goes unpunished. Remember this when you hear someone talking about your leadership as a Sunday school teacher, an elder, a deacon, or a Vacation Bible School director. Outside of church this happens all the time in the workplace. If you need help being wise in such circumstances, Solomon gives you some good advice: remember how *you* talked about the one who was over you. Paul later generalizes that each Christian ought "not to think of himself more highly than he ought to think, but to think with sober judgment" (Rom. 12:4). Solomon gives us a concrete circumstance in which to do this. Love covers a multitude of sins.

Thus, wisdom does not consist in power ("ten rulers"), but in recognizing one's own limitations and sins, and in learning to rule over our "servants" in a way that is consistent with our own self-awareness of sin. The wise man has discovered the ineradicable sinfulness of man and he has learned to deal with people in the light of this truth. Too often, we live in a dream world. We are surprised to discover that someone we love and respect is a sinner! He or she fails us. It may be our husband or wife, our elder or pastor, our good friend or neighbor. Sooner or later you will discover that he or she, like you, is a sinner. They will fail you. They will surprise you.

To get us out of the dream world, Solomon presents us with the Biblical realism of Christian wisdom. You cannot relinquish confidence in a man, woman, leader, pastor, or elder just because they erred! Christian wisdom reflects carefully on the "stupidity of wickedness and the madness of folly" (7:25c; NIV), and then acts accordingly without writing people off. If you try so desperately to be correct on every score, if you ignore the fact of human sinfulness, you will inevitably hear every word as a criticism of yourself. Be careful not to become so sensitive to what others say that even the words of subordinates are taken too seriously. The heart of sinners—our hearts—are constantly bubbling up with curses and bitterness (Rom. 3:14). Do you know your own heart? Or are you ignorant of your own sinfulness? If you are wise about yourself you will overlook faults in others.

Solomon continues (7:23) that he has tested "all this" by wisdom. By "all this," he is referring to everything in verses nineteen through twenty-two, specifically the value of wisdom in a fallen world where even the righteous man sins. The value of such wisdom has been shown practically in the example of verses twenty-one and twenty-two. But its value lies precisely in its willingness to admit its limitations. Figuring out the reasons for sin, for backbiting, and for the sins that the righteous commit—"that which has been" (cf. 1:9)—is beyond his power to understand. It is "far off," "deep," and beyond finding out (7:24).

There are other aspects of the sinful world that Solomon can comment upon. Reiterating his use of wisdom to understand evil (7:25), Solomon considers "the woman." This passage is not a polemic against women in general, nor even about certain types of women. The text clearly speaks of "the woman" in a way that is definitive. We are expected to know to which woman Solomon refers.

In the wisdom literature of Solomon there are always two women—the adulterous woman and the virtuous woman. Each stands for folly and wisdom respectively. Here "the woman" is "folly" (which is a feminine noun in the Hebrew). This deadly seductress lures a man away from wisdom's embrace. She is the "other woman," the opposite of Lady Wisdom. This deadly seducer (folly) is set over against wisdom, the one who protects and watches and gives life (Prov. 1:20–33; 3:13–18; 4:5–13; 8:1–31). With handcuffs for hands and a heart like a steel trap, we have a powerful metaphor of the deadly seductive power of wickedness and folly. This passage then is not advice to young men about dating, but rather a warning to all men and women to follow faithfulness and pursue lady wisdom. Foolishness and wickedness are out on a hunt, trying to lure and trap people and lead them down a deadly path. Everyone is vulnerable, *specifically the one who considers himself invulnerable.*

> The woman Folly is loud;
>   she is seductive and knows nothing.
> She sits at the door of her house;
>   she takes a seat on the highest places of the town,
> calling to those who pass by,
>   who are going straight on their way,
> "Whoever is simple, let him turn in here!"
>   And to him who lacks sense she says,
> "Stolen water is sweet,
>   and bread eaten in secret is pleasant."
> But he does not know that the dead are there,
>   that her guests are in the depths of Sheol. (Prov. 9:13–18)

The shepherd king now tells us what he has "seen"—that is, what he has wisely *discerned*. He uses the language of math in describing his attempts to understand "while adding one thing to another" (7:27). No matter how hard you try, no matter what kind of accounting you may give, people cannot be thoroughly searched out—they cannot be understood. Human beings, particularly sinful human beings, are beyond searching out. They are mysterious.

They say things and do things that are enigmatic and irrational. They are *hebel*. Vaporous.

Verse twenty-eight has given Solomon an undeserved reputation as a misogynist. He is not saying that he can't find any woman, let alone any upright woman (contrary to the NIV, the word "upright" is not in the text). He is not saying that he can only find one man in a thousand. Rather, he is saying he can't *understand* them. Being "found" here means, as elsewhere in the book of Ecclesiastes, to be fathomed or understood. Solomon is simply saying that he can *figure out* one man in a thousand, but not women. Human beings are mysterious and the opposite sex is all the more so.

Systematic, comprehensive understanding of particular men and women is elusive and enigmatic. The human person—particularly the depraved, fallen human person—will not yield itself to your investigations. Fallen man himself is vapor or mist.

Solomon set on a quest for a quantification (7:27). Like a clerk or an accountant, the pastor runs his finger down the inventory of man's life, item by item, "one by one," to look for a pattern, a reason, a comprehensive accounting for what this person is and does. It eludes him. Why? Sin is insane; wickedness is moronic and stupid (7:25). It makes no sense.

The explanation of the mystery of human nature is articulated in verse twenty-nine: "See, this alone *I found*, that God made man upright, but *they have sought out* many schemes" (emphasis added). Man's fall into sin leaves us surrounded by mystery. Unfallen man, made in God's image, would also be mysterious, no doubt, but sin adds to the incomprehensible complexity of human nature. We might call this Solomon's "ignorance doctrine."

This, incidentally, is the key new idea that concludes this third section (chapters 6 through 8). "Then I saw all the work of God, that man *cannot find out* the work that is done under the sun. However much man may toil in seeking, *he will not find it out*. Even though a wise man claims to know, *he cannot find it out*" (8:17; emphasis added). For now, Solomon ends with a note of triumph about wisdom, saying that it makes the possessor's face glow and takes away its hardness.

It seems that to attain this insight—this ignorance doctrine—is in some sense to know the ultimate explanation. In this case, the ultimate explanation for life is that ultimate explanations, precise accountings for others or even for our own behavior, elude us all. It means that your face can shine. You can live life without all the answers, without an exact accounting of everything and everyone. And, as we shall see (8:2ff), it ought to lead you to humble submission to the authorities that God has placed over you.

THE RIDDLES OF RULING A COMMUNITY

A few years ago when my younger children were smaller, I saw this plastic outdoor table and I thought it would be great for them to play with outdoors. It was a little picnic table with two compartments in it. One was for water and the other was for sand. I had visions of how much they would enjoy this. They could build little sand castles or play with toy soldiers with sand fortifications, then they could sail toy boats in the water. They would love it, I thought, as they went from one compartment to the other.

So I bought the table and filled one side with water so they had a little pool they could sit at. I went out and purchased some sand for the other compartment. How long to do you think the sand and the water stayed where each was supposed to go?

People are never as manageable as their managers think they should be. I had a vision of how I wanted my children to have fun, but my children didn't consult me as to how I wanted them to act. I tried to learn from this experience how uncontrollable children are. Wisdom dictates that if you are called to parent children, you actually parent real children, not imaginary ones.

People are complicated. Not only are they made in the image of the infinite and inexhaustible God, but they are twisted by sin. All of this makes the issues of ruling over others a hard one to figure out. We are fallen and those whom we are charged to obey are fallen, depraved humans as well. Excuses abound both for tyranny and rebellion.

Solomon brings this third section to a close with some admonitions and observations concerning human society, specifically how the riddle of fallen humanity—the mystery of depraved man—affects the order of rule and subjection in the human community. It shouldn't surprise us that Solomon, as a king, should instruct us in godly rule and submission. This is a major theme in Solomonic wisdom literature. It has theological bearing for all Christians, for God declares us to be kings enthroned with his son (Rev. 1:6; 6:10; Eph. 2:6).

The unfathomable evil of humanity (end of chapter 7) demands a social order with authority and submission, kings and subjects, rulers and ruled. Rulers are charged with maintaining God's order so that human society can be free to flourish. Those who are subjects are charged with obedience and submission to the complex of authorities in any human community—parents, church officers, civil governors, masters-employers. This is God's gracious arrangement. Though it is not and was never intended to eradicate the evil of humanity, at least this kind of arrangement can guard from anarchy and chaos. More to the point, the evil in the world is no excuse for rebellion or despair. Faith looks to God's final judgment for ultimate and exacting justice.

There are four stages in Solomon's teaching in 8:2–17.

1. Solomon gives a general admonition to wise, godly submission (8:2–7).
2. Solomon gives a reminder of the limitations and evil of human governors (8:8–10).
3. There is an exhortation to fear God and exercise faith in the Lord's final judgment (8:11–14).
4. Finally, Solomon concludes the third section (6:1–8:17) with the now-familiar encouragement to receive God's good gifts without trying to figure everything out (8:15–17).

First, we learn of the *need for wise, godly submission to authority.* For Solomon, in this passage, respectful submission is the order of the day. This is a difficult admonition to heed, but the Bible as a whole requires submission to those placed in authority over us. With very few exceptions, kings, governors, rules, elders, parents, and other authorities are to be obeyed, even when you disagree, even when you think they are wrong, *even* when they are wicked.

> I say: Keep the king's command, because of God's oath to him. Be not hasty to go from his presence. Do not take your stand in an evil cause, for he does whatever he pleases. For the word of the king is supreme, and who may say to him, "What are you doing?" Whoever keeps a command will know no evil thing, and the wise heart will know the proper time and the just way. For there is a time and a way for everything, although man's trouble lies heavy on him. For he does not know what is to be, for who can tell him how it will be. (Eccl. 8:2–7)

Whether the oath here mentioned (8:2) is one that a king has taken before God in such a way that his kingship is given divine authority, or whether it is some kind of oath of allegiance taken by the subjects—whatever the case may be—what is clear is that subjection to the governing authorities is given a religious basis. It is a matter of conscience. Obey your superiors after the manner of an oath before God.

That the king acts in God's place is evidenced by the fact that his word is authoritative and should not be questioned (8:4). The same language here is used of the way creatures must respond to God himself (Isa. 29:16; 64:8; Jer. 18:6). The word used here for the king's commandment (*mitsvah*) is the word normally associated with divine commandments. The human authorities that are in place are there according to God's institution and they act on God's behalf as his ministers. This fits well with the apostle Paul's teaching that you must be subject to the governing authorities, not merely for the sake of "wrath" but also for conscience's sake (Rom. 13:5).

Of course, there is also a practical reason—escaping punishment. Nevertheless, we must not lose sight of the profound theological reason, if you want to obey God you will submit to the leaders he has put over you. The true basis for all faithful subjection to authority is that God speaks and acts and commands *through* them. Romans 13:1 spells this out rather clearly, even calling the magistrates God's ministers. Instinctively, readers want to think that this is only true of godly rulers, but that is not Solomon's wisdom nor Paul's doctrine. The apostle instructs Titus in the teaching of his people: "Remind them to be submissive to rulers and authorities, to be obedient, to be ready for every good work, to speak evil of no one, to avoid quarreling, to be gentle, and to show perfect courtesy toward all people" (Titus 3:1–2). The rationale Paul offers shows that these rulers are anything but godly: "For we ourselves were once foolish, disobedient, led astray, slaves to various passions and pleasures, passing our days in malice and envy, hated by others and hating one another" (Titus 3:3). Plainly, this duty of deference, obedience, and submission extends even to wicked masters and bad kings.

Solomon writes that "whoever keeps a command will know no evil thing" (8:5a). Obviously Solomon knows of evil tyrants who destroy those who have done nothing contrary to their commands. The "evil thing" here is not simply suffering but the suffering one deserves for rebelling against God's rulers (cf. Rom. 13:2–4).

Solomon points out that understanding the right way to respond to authority requires discernment (8:5b–6a). The wise will learn to be discreet and discern the proper time and place. Responding to authority is an *art*. Grudging obedience can never be the norm, but rather cheerful compliance (8:3: "Be not hasty to go from his presence"). This wisdom can be learned and practiced despite the curse, "the evil of humanity," (ESV: "man's trouble") and despite the limitations of wisdom (8:6b–7).

Children have such a hard time getting this right precisely because they are immature. They go about dealing with their parents in the wrong way and then are rebuked. Thus, they get the false impression that they have no way to be heard, no voice, no way to talk to their parents about decisions that are made! It is precisely when they mature that they grasp the right way to appeal to authority.

Next, Solomon deals with the limitations that are over rulers:

> No man has power to retain the spirit, or power over the day of death. There is no discharge from war, nor will wickedness deliver those who are given to it. All this I observed while applying my heart to all that is done under the sun, when man had power over man to his hurt. Then I saw the wicked buried. They used to go in and out of the holy place and were praised in the city where they had done such things. This also is [vapor]. (8:8–10)

Despite what has been said above, rulers would be stupid to think their powers are unlimited. If parents often can't manage their children, how much more are men or women unable to manage the big issues of society and nations? People in authority are tempted with visions of godhood and divinity. Rulers must remember they are only human. "No man has power to retain the spirit, or power over the day of death" (Eccl. 8:8a). Subjects must remember, too, that their rulers are fallen people who may err in their edicts, laws, and sanctions.

Good rulers will always recognize this fact. King Canute ruled in England from 1016–1035, arriving there as a pagan but dying as a Christian king of Denmark, Norway, and England. At one point he erected his throne before the rising tide to demonstrate that as a human king he could not hold back the ocean's waves. Thus he dramatically taught his subjects that although he had his authority from God, he was not god himself.

In verses eight and nine Solomon seems to be saying that the godly ruler knows all too well his limitations and impotence with regard to his subjects. The wise ruler will discern a proper time and judgment for every matter, even though he appreciates the "evil of humanity" and the fact that his power extends only so far. Wickedness cannot be legislated out of existence. Life or obedience cannot be poured into another human being because rulers are given "no power to retain the spirit." This is very instructive for all of us who have positions of authority over others—parents, managers, alderman, representatives, policeman, pastors, elders, Sunday school teachers. We can't make people do what we want. Social engineering always goes haywire. Our government over other humans must be tempered with wisdom and humility.

In verse ten there arises this crisis for the believer: you must obey the governing authorities, but you can't trust them as God because you know their limitations and corruption. So when you see and experience the contradiction, what do you do? You fear God and trust his promise.

These observations, then, lead naturally into *an exhortation to fear God and exercise faith in his final judgment* (8:11–14). Solomon has pointed out that the political situation is uncontrollable by man. It is vapor. We can easily see how this might lead people to become paralyzed with fear and foreboding. This feeling results in the idea that *everything* is a conspiracy and that the sky is falling. The fact that life is out of one's control tempts a person to think someone else must be in control, that the wicked are ruling with absolute control and competence. Political activists are aware that people feel this way and exploit it. You probably get several direct mail appeals in your mailbox every week announcing a new threat, a new law that will bring down civilization, or a new conspiracy. Solomon points out that paranoia and paralysis are not the proper stance in life.

> Because the sentence against an evil deed is not executed speedily, the heart of the children of man is fully set to do evil. Though a sinner does evil a hundred times and prolongs his life, yet I know that it will be well with those who fear God, because they fear before him. But it will not be well with the wicked, neither will he prolong his days like a shadow, because he does not fear before God.
>
> There is a [vapor] that takes place on earth, that there are righteous people to whom it happens according to the deeds of the wicked, and there are wicked people to whom it happens according to the deeds of the righteous. I said that this also is [vapor]. (8:11–14)

Verse eleven is not so much a proof text for quick trials and speedy execution of civil sentences. The emphasis is on the foolish deduction that the wicked make from the delay of punishment.

People dare to do more evil just because sentence is delayed. This is how stupid fallen man is. This is how we think! A criminal thinks he's going to get away with it. People dare to push the envelop of evil just because nothing seems to be happening to them. They appear to be getting away with it.

In fact, in biblical justice, delaying punishment is actually a merciful space for the criminal. It gives him time to repent (Rom. 2:2–4). Tragically, people take the opposite direction: "But if that wicked servant says to himself, 'My master is delayed,' and begins to beat his fellow servants and eats and drinks with drunkards, the master of that servant will come on a day when he does not expect him and at an hour he does not know and will cut him in pieces and put him with the hypocrites. In that place there will be weeping and gnashing of teeth" (Matt. 24:48–51).

Like Jesus, Solomon makes it very clear that judgment awaits those who think that that they can get away with evil in human society. If judicial sentence is delayed or even derailed that does not mean that people get off scot-free. This is why it is so important for a society to have a kind of corporate Christian conscience. Without a conviction of God's judgment on the last day, there are no restraints on wickedness other than the civil punishments inflicted by the civil authorities. And without a societal conviction that God will administer perfect justice at the last day and correct what went wrong in human history, then the state must become godlike and seek to spy on everyone, regulate all of life, and punish every little infraction.

Furthermore, in such a society people must take matters into their own hands when they feel that they have not been given judgment. No one can rest in God's future judgment. We must litigate everything so that we can get justice now. The gospel gives us freedom from vendettas and tyrants: "Therefore do not pronounce judgment before the time, before the Lord comes, who will bring to light the things now hidden in darkness and will disclose the purposes of the heart. Then each one will receive his commendation from God" (1 Cor. 4:5). "Repay no one evil for evil, but give thought to do what is honorable in the sight of all. If possible, so far as it depends on you, live peaceably with all. Beloved, never avenge yourselves, but leave it to the wrath of God, for it is written, 'Vengeance is mine, I will repay, says the Lord' " (Rom. 12:17–19).

The judgment of the wicked is in God's hands. Just because "a sinner does evil a hundred times and prolongs his life" does not mean there is no reason to "fear God" (8:12). The quest for justice is vapor to us. It is even vapor to rulers, judges, kings, and lawmakers. By faith you should hold fast to the promise that God will judge men and nations and that they will not get away with great crimes. Even if there is no poetic justice on earth, in history, God promises there will be at history's end. Indeed, this is one of Solomon's final, concluding assertions at the end of the book. "For God will bring every deed into judgment, with every secret thing, whether good or evil" (Eccl. 12:14).

Finally, Solomon gives us an encouragement to receive God's good gifts without trying to figure everything out. At the conclusion of each of Solomon's four sections we have the dual admonition to *fear God* and *enjoy the food and drink and other good gifts that he gives us*. This conclusion is true to the pattern.

> And I commend joy, for man has no good thing under the sun but to eat and drink and be joyful, for this will go with him in his toil through the days of his life that God has given him under the sun.
>
> When I applied my heart to know wisdom, and to see the business that is done on earth, how neither day nor night do one's eyes see sleep, then I saw all the work of God, that man cannot find out the work that is done under the sun. However much man may toil in seeking, he will not find it out. Even though a wise man claims to know, he cannot find it out. (8:15–17)

What is distinctive about this ending is the emphasis on our need to realize that it is impossible to figure everything out. Winston Churchill was not speaking of God when he made his now-famous quip, but it's perfectly suited to describe what we have been learning here in Ecclesiastes: "a riddle wrapped in a mystery inside an enigma." In the last verse (8:17), Solomon uses the same Hebrew word three times to emphasize that no one can "find out" what God is doing in history. "Figure out" might be more helpful to understanding what he is saying. God's ways are higher than our ways, his thoughts beyond searching out.

This realization need not paralyze anyone, especially Christians. After all, we trust God even though we cannot comprehend his ways with us. Since we are creatures and for that reason entirely dependent on the Lord, we should relax and enjoy the good gifts he bestows on us. Enjoying what God has given you to enjoy and abstaining from trying to figure out the injustice and tyranny in the world are two things that go together not only in Solomon's writing here but also in Paul's letters. He urges the Thessalonians, for example, "to aspire to live quietly, and to mind your own affairs, and to work with your hands, as we instructed you." He also lays down a rule for his congregations.

> First of all, then, I urge that supplications, prayers, intercessions, and thanksgivings be made for all people, for kings and all who are in high positions, that we may lead a peaceful and quiet life, godly and dignified in every way. This is good, and it is pleasing in the sight of God our Savior. (1 Tim. 3:1–2)

Part Four

Ecclesiastes 9–12

Solomon's language changes a bit in this last section. For one thing, he shifts from the investigative mode of discourse to something more definitive. Now we primarily have the exaltation of the primacy of wisdom and advice, judgments, and commands. Note the way chapter 8 ends and chapter 9 begins. At the conclusion of chapter 8 Solomon speaks of observing "all the work of God," noting how one cannot exhaustively "find it out" (8:17). Then he begins chapter 9 with a reference to "all this" (9:1). Solomon is coming to the end, preparing to comment on everything he has observed.

Even so, the riddle-like character of the book becomes even more marked in the final installment of Solomon's presentation. This should not surprise us. The lessons of wise men cannot be transmitted in simplistic maxims. That would be much too superficial and untrue to the complexities of life.

This final movement in Ecclesiastes can be outlined and summarized as follows:

9:1–10:20	If everything is vapor, does that include wisdom? Is wisdom immune to the *hebel*-ness of life? Does wisdom work like some sort of magic key that unlocks the secrets of this vaporous life and makes everything work out all right? If you are a wise man or woman, will you rise above the vaporous quality of life under the sun? Will you get relief from chasing after the wind? With wisdom can you leverage things in order to escape the curse and death? No. Solomon finally commends the superiority of wisdom; but he cannot do so without seriously qualifying his commendation. This is probably the overarching lesson of this section—wisdom's superiority, yet vulnerability. Wisdom is a God-given gift that will bring you success in this life—*limited* success. Wise men and women are vulnerable, too. There are always flies in the ointment. Everybody sins. Everybody dies.

11:1–6 Next we learn what Solomon meant when earlier in the book when he encouraged us to "do good" (3:12). What is this "labor" or "work" that Solomon has been cryptically commending to us in his mini-conclusions? Recall that he was searching for what was most beneficial for man to do: "I searched in my heart . . . till I might see what was *good* for the sons of men to *do* under heaven all the days of their lives" (2:3). Now Solomon makes it plain—relatively plain, at any rate. It is still couched in language that only the wise will be able to discern, but the lesson of the first six verses of chapter 11 is crucial for understanding the conclusion of the book. *Despite life's vaporous uncontrollability and even wisdom's vulnerability, the Creator promises ultimate fulfillment when his people trust him and venture to serve others.* Go ahead. Take the risk. Cast your bread upon the waters.

11:7–12:14 Solomon concludes with a summons to the young man to enjoy light and sweetness. Enjoy the years that God gives you, take advantage of your youth, and follow your heart. The days of darkness will come, disquieting days without pleasure. As he has said before, death awaits us all. Now he paints a somber picture of the final days of an old, dying man (12:2–8). In this realistic portrayal of old age and approaching death, we encounter a succession of images of distortion and despair. Anyone who has witnessed an elderly relative's last days before death will know exactly what Solomon says here. One day we will experience it, too. After this, Solomon concludes his book with observations about book-writing, the words of the wise, their relation to the divine Shepherd King, and a final call to fear God and keep his commandments.

10

Wine, Oil, and a Few Flies: Ecclesiastes 9:1–10:20

You cause the grass to grow for the livestock and plants
for man to cultivate, that he may bring forth food from the earth
and wine to gladden the heart of man, oil to make his face shine
and bread to strengthen man's heart. —Psalm 104:14–1

As I worked on this chapter, the media were filled with updates on the aftermath of Hurricane Katrina and the estimated hundreds of dead bodies floating in the floodwaters from the Mississippi. I can only pray that, by the time you read this, somehow it will turn out that the loss of life was overestimated.

Hundreds, maybe thousands, are dead who, a couple of weeks earlier, were looking forward to long lives. Even if the estimated death toll turns out to be exaggerated, the storm has brought a kind of death even to those who have lived through the calamity. Many people lost close to everything. All their hopes and dreams are revealed as vapor. It is amazing to think how much money and labor went into the construction of Interstate 10 and how much history and culture were behind New Orleans. Yet Interstate 10 is now in pieces and New Orleans has become a lake, all because of one storm that no one could control. The results of all that effort and energy are suddenly brought to an end.

When death and destruction happen on such a grand scale, we are almost numbed to the significance of it, but on a smaller scale, it happens all the time. During the time I was preaching through Ecclesiastes to my congregation, a drunk driver killed the bride of one of my friends from the army. This was a man with whom I had shared Christian fellowship. They both seemed meant for each other and had been married only about a year. He had moved to Arizona with her to start a new career and a new life together and then a drunk driver plowed his vehicle into hers. All their plans and labors were vapor.

Solomon now returns to the heart of the matter here in chapter 9. He has investigated under the guidance of God's Spirit the length and depth and breadth of human existence in the first eight chapters. Now we are reminded of the chief manifestation of the *hebel-ness*, the *vaporous* character of human existence: death, together with all the frustration one experiences in the face of the great leveler. Life is best lived not by denying the reality of death, but by understanding one's place in this life and living by faith.

> But all this I laid to heart, examining it all, how the righteous and the wise and their deeds are in the hand of God. Whether it is love or hate, man does not know; both are before him. It is the same for all, since the same event happens to the righteous and the wicked, to the good and the evil, to the clean and the unclean, to him who sacrifices and him who does not sacrifice. As is the good, so is the sinner, and he who swears is as he who shuns an oath. This is an evil in all that is done under the sun, that the same event happens to all. Also, the hearts of the children of man are full of evil, and madness is in their hearts while they live, and after that they go to the dead. But he who is joined with all the

> living has hope, for a living dog is better than a dead lion. For the living know that they will die, but the dead know nothing, and they have no more reward, for the memory of them is forgotten. Their love and their hate and their envy have already perished, and forever they have no more share in all that is done under the sun. (Eccl. 9:1–6)

All mortals face the common curse of evil under the sun; this is most pointedly obvious in the inescapability of death. Solomon is centered on how life can be lived in the face of this great evil. His concern for life (as opposed to death) is shown by the way he balances three references to "life" in the first section (9:4–5) with three answering references in the second section (9:9). Indeed, Solomon is clear that death is not to be preferred to life. Notice that the dead have no "share" or "portion," whereas the living do (9:6, 9; the Hebrew uses the same word). Solomon is advocating a vigorous engagement with life, not a stoic resignation to the inevitability of fate.

In the first verse Solomon states his thesis: we are all in God's hands, the righteous and the wise and everything they do. This, he says, is the result of his investigation. While this is a basis for understanding our need to trust in God, it is also disconcerting. The fact that the righteous and the wise are in God's hands means that their own hands are impotent to control their lives. Indeed, verse two states that this means the wise and the righteous and all their works are in the same situation as the wicked. Everyone dies. The future is unknowable and uncontrollable. We do not and cannot know the mind of God for the particulars of our lives, but one thing is sure. The curse of death is universally experienced.

This is a call to faith, as the whole book of Ecclesiastes is a call to faith. It is one that we modern westerners especially need to heed. As Americans we are consumed with predicting and controlling the future. We seem to think, paradoxically, that our prosperity is a sign of God's favor and that we ourselves must have godlike powers over the future in order to maintain our lives, but both ideas are false. We don't have such powers and our level of prosperity does not tell us anything about what God thinks of us.

"Whether it is love or hate, man does not know" (9:1). This statement probably means that one cannot discern God's love or hatred from the outward circumstances of one's life. This is one of the minor themes in Ecclesiastes. Since the same fate awaits the fool as well as the wise man, how can you divine God's favor from what you experience in this life? Doesn't everyone die?

One cannot discern or know from one's experience whether health or sickness, wealth or poverty, life or death is solid evidence of God's love or displeasure. Experience cannot decide. God's ways with man are inscrutable. God's freedom is unbounded in this life. We cannot tell by God's treatment of particular individuals whether they are objects of God's love or hatred.

Solomon is following his own argument. He warned in Ecclesiastes 6:1–6 that prosperity is not always a good thing and in 7:1–15 that adversity and affliction are not always purely evil. Elsewhere, Solomon also teaches that "better is a dinner of herbs where love is than a fattened ox and hatred with it" (Prov. 15:17). Eating poorly can be preferable to eating one's fill because there are *other factors to consider*. We must remember Job's friends. They looked at the facts and concluded that Job was being punished, that God's favor had been removed from him because he had concealed some evil behavior. But suffering proves nothing. Suffering can be (1) educational/for chastisement (Heb. 12:3–11); (2) doxological (John 9:1–3); (3) probationary (Habbakuk); (4) revelational (Hosea); (5) sacrificial (Jesus; even Paul, Col. 1:24–25); (6) punishment (Rev. 2:21–23); or for some reason entirely inscrutable to us (Job 1–2).

While Solomon claims that there is no figuring out God's attitude and waxes poetic about how everyone meets the same fate (9:2–3), he is clear that there is a universal reason for this universal situation: all men and women, no matter what their age, station, or abilities, are evil. "The hearts of the children of man are full of evil, and madness is in their hearts while they live, and after that they go to the dead" (Eccl. 9:3). Again, this is something that Solomon has already established (7:20).

While all men and women are equal as far as their destiny in this world, that does not mean that it makes no difference whether they are alive or dead (9:4). The living have hope. This hope is the trust, the faith, which the living have in God. If you are still alive, there is this hope of preparation for meeting God, hope of living significantly, hope of doing something for the glory of God before all men meet him personally face to face. As Solomon will say later, "For God will bring every deed into judgment, with every secret thing, whether good or evil" (12:14).

Paul wrote that Christians must walk, "making the best use of the time, because the days are evil" (Eph. 5:16). Solomon concurs (9:5). The irony is that the living know that they are going to die. This is the advantage of the living. They can live in the light of that certainty. It should motivate them to enjoy life rather than pin their hopes on attaining some sort of ultimate advantage. Solomon does not deny conscious existence after death. This is not a denial of any hope for life after death. His point is the same as Paul's and the same as Jesus's when Jesus told his disciples, "We must work the works of him who sent me while it is day; night is coming, when no one can work" (John 9:24). The fact is that whatever joys await a Christian after death, they are not the same things we enjoy now, under the sun. Once you are dead those joys and other experiences are all gone. Appreciate what you have while you have it.

How can you enjoy life and be glad when you cannot tell God's attitude toward you? If the blessings you have do not mean that God loves you, if the curses you suffer *might* indicate that you are under God's curse, then how can you not worry about these things? The answer is not to look for signs of God's favor in our common life under the sun, but rather to listen to the Word of God. Do you want to know what God thinks of you? Is that important to you? Well, then, *let Solomon tell you*: "God has already approved what you do" (9:7). Believe the gospel. You are righteous in God's sight. Solomon is teaching us justification by faith. Indeed, he is teaching us justification by faith apart from works, for those are all vapor. It is only by faith that we can say that God has accepted them.

> Go, eat your bread in joy, and drink your wine with a merry heart, for God has already approved what you do.

> Let your garments be always white. Let not oil be lacking on your head.
>
> Enjoy life with the wife whom you love, all the days of your [vaporous] life that he has given you under the sun, because that is your portion in life and in your toil at which you toil under the sun. Whatever your hand finds to do, do it with your might, for there is no work or thought or knowledge or wisdom in Sheol, to which you are going. (9:7–10)

Solomon's declaration that God has accepted our works is central to verses seven and eight. Solomon gives us four commands: eat bread, drink wine, wear white, and oil your head. In the middle of those four commands, between the wine and the garments, he tells us that we are accepted. Justification is the central reason why we can and must confidently do these things.

What Solomon lists here are essential gospel images. The bread and wine is the one rite Christ established for normal Christian worship—the Lord's Supper. Being clothed in white represents being clothed in salvation (Rev. 3:4–5, 18; 19:14), and anointing is something all Christians have received (2 Cor. 1:21; 1 John 2:27). Obviously, to some extent, oil on the head is hard for us to relate to, but just think of shampoo on your head. Remember how it makes you feel. It is as if Solomon were to say to us, "Use that apple-scented shampoo that smells so good and wear bright and cheery clothes." Is your stomach knotted up from stress and worry about your health? Drink some wine, as Paul advises Timothy (1 Tim. 5:23).

Solomon is telling us that that it is God's will in Christ that we enjoy the basic provisions of life that he has given us. He is the one who provides them for us. He accepts—indeed, commands—our participation in the enjoyment of life, food, marriage, and work. So go ahead and do as God would want! Eat, drink, love, and work. God has accepted these activities. The mark of a biblical wise man or woman is that despite the many painful issues in life—namely, death—the wise are able to enjoy life as a gift of God. They know when pleasure and feasting and love are appropriate.

Not only do they enjoy the little luxuries God provides, but they also make a point of enjoying their callings in work and marriage. Just as each Israelite family received a specific piece of property in the Promised Land according to the casting of a lot (in which God controlled the outcome), so marriage and work are your "lot" or "portion" in life from God (9:9). Since there is a great deal of unholy prudery in the church, I'm going to say it plainly. Christian spouses are supposed to enjoy life by enjoying sex with each other and all the other blessings of marriage. Solomon is not giving us some form of hedonistic nihilism here. He is not saying eat, drink, and be merry, for tomorrow we die. He is saying we should receive the good things in life as gifts from God because that is what they are.

This is not some denial of what Solomon has said about all people being leveled by death, but rather the proper response to it on the part of a mature believer. He should be able to enjoy life without deceiving himself about having some sort of advantage or leverage through his work or his wisdom. The very way Solomon structures this passage demonstrates that he is keeping his vision focused on the way the world really is even while he makes these confessions of faith. Notice how he returns in verses eleven and twelve to what he has already stated in verses two and three:

> Again I saw that under the sun the race is not to the swift, nor the battle to the strong, nor bread to the wise, nor riches to the intelligent, nor favor to those with knowledge, but time and chance happen to them all. For man does not know his time. Like fish that are taken in an evil net, and like birds that are caught in a snare, so the children of man are snared at an evil time, when it suddenly falls upon them. (9:11–12)

This section begins and ends with death as the universal constant, but still assures us that we should value life (9:4–6) and enjoy life (9:7–10).

While studying Ecclesiastes, I was enrolled as a graduate student at a Lutheran seminary. I came across this advice from Luther while doing research for a paper. Luther wrote to Jerome Weller in 1530 about how to conquer various temptations.

> In this sort of temptation and struggle, contempt is the best and easiest method of winning over the devil. Laugh your adversary to scorn and ask who it is with whom you are talking. But by all means flee solitude, for the devil watches and lies in wait for you most of all when you are alone. This devil is conquered by mocking and despising him, not by resisting and arguing with him. Therefore, Jerome, joke and play games with your wife and others. In this way you will drive out your diabolical thoughts and take courage. . . .
>
> Be of good courage, therefore, and cast these dreadful thoughts out of your mind. Whenever the devil pesters you with these thoughts, at once seek out the company of other Christian men, drink more, joke and jest, or engage in some other form of merriment. Sometimes it is necessary to drink a little more, play, jest, or even commit some infraction in defiance and contempt. Accordingly if the devil should say, "Do not drink," you should reply to him, "On this very account, because you forbid it, I shall drink, and what is more, I shall drink a generous amount." Thus one must always do the opposite of that which Satan prohibits. What do you think is my reason for drinking wine undiluted, talking freely, and eating more often, if it is not to torment and vex the devil who made up his mind to torment and vex me.

Luther wrote similar advice in a letter to Prince Joachim of Anhalt (1534) who suffered from melancholy and "dejection of spirit."

> I should like to encourage Your Grace, who are a young man, always to be joyful, to engage in riding and hunting, and to seek the company of others who may be able to rejoice with Your Grace in a godly and honorable way. For solitude and inwardness are poisonous and deadly to all people, and especially to a young man. Accordingly, God has commanded us to be joyful in his presence; he does not desire a gloomy sacrifice. [Luther quotes Ecclesiastes 12.] No one realizes how much harm it does a young person to avoid pleasure and cultivate solitude and sadness. Your grace has Master Nicholas Hausman and many others near at hand. Be merry with them; for gladness and good cheer, when decent and proper, are the best medicine for a young person—indeed, for all people. I myself, who have spent a good part of my life in sorrow and gloom, now seek and find joy wherever I can. Praise God, we now have sufficient understanding of the Word of

> God to be able to rejoice with a good conscience and to use God's gifts with thanksgiving, for he created them for this purpose and is pleased when we use them. (Theodore G. Tappert, ed., *Luther: Letters of Spiritual Counsel* [Philadelphia: Westminster Press, 1960], 92–93)

According to Solomon, Luther possessed and dispensed true wisdom.

FLIES IN THE OINTMENT

Becoming wise and mature often consists in simply being able to acknowledge and negotiate the *complexity* of life, that several different things are true. That is why our folk wisdom in America can easily be shown to contradict itself. Various sayings encourage the opposite sort of behavior from other sayings; for example, "Nothing ventured, nothing gained" and "A bird in the hand is worth two in the bush." Many other examples could be listed. Such statements are both true, though in different contexts. A person is wise not simply by affirming the sayings but by acquiring the discernment to know when and where one of them applies.

This is why it is extremely hard to teach wisdom with mere verbal communication. Wisdom demands that people grasp *both*, but unwise ears or eyes seem able to only hear or read one or the other. Trying to verbally communicate wisdom almost *demands* that the communicator put opposite statements together as riddles to stump the audience. Otherwise, if someone tries to teach truths and then qualify what he has said, invariably he finds he must turn around and again qualify his qualifications!

Solomon almost seems to be in that sort of situation. By now you should be able to figure out what Solomon will say about the value and the advantage of wisdom. Right? Wisdom is superior. Wisdom is valuable. "The beginning of wisdom is this: get wisdom, and whatever you get, get insight" (Prov. 4:7).

But a question arises: Is wisdom immune to the *hebel*-ness of life? Is wisdom some sort of magic key that unlocks the secrets of this vaporous life and makes everything work out all right? If you are a wise man or woman will you rise above the vaporous quality of life under the sun? Will you get relief from your attempt to shepherd the wind? Can you escape sin and death? No. Solomon has been clear on this. Remember what he said at the beginning:

> I the Preacher have been king over Israel in Jerusalem. And I applied my heart to seek and to search out by wisdom all that is done under heaven. It is an unhappy business that God has given to the children of man to be busy with. I have seen everything that is done under the sun, and behold, all is [vapor] and [shepherding the wind].
>
> What is crooked cannot be made straight,
> and what is lacking cannot be counted.
>
> I said in my heart, "I have acquired great wisdom, surpassing all who were over Jerusalem before me, and my heart has had great experience of wisdom and knowledge." And I applied my heart to know wisdom and to know madness and folly. I perceived that this also is but [shepherding the wind].
>
> For in much wisdom is much vexation,
> and he who increases knowledge
> increases sorrow. (Eccl. 1:12–18)

Solomon finally commends the superiority of wisdom, but he cannot do so without seriously qualifying his commendation. Wisdom is a god-given gift that will bring you *limited* success in this life. Wise men and women are vulnerable, too. This is probably the overarching lesson of this section: wisdom's superiority, yet vulnerability. While the connection between all of these sayings can be difficult to discern, I think they all have to do with this dialectic, this polarity between the superiority and the liabilities of wisdom.

> I have also seen this example of wisdom under the sun, and it seemed great to me. There was a little city with few men in it, and a great king came against it and besieged it, building great siege works against it. But there was found in it a poor, wise man, and he

> by his wisdom delivered the city. Yet no one remembered that poor man. But I say that wisdom is better than might, though the poor man's wisdom is despised and his words are not heard. (9:13–16)

Solomon lays it out pretty unambiguously right up front with this story. In this illustrative account he admits that to be wise is to possess practical knowledge that enables the man or woman to achieve success. In Proverbs, Solomon shows that this is a godly and godlike virtue: "Yahweh by wisdom founded the earth; by understanding he established the heavens" (Prov. 3:19). Indeed, elsewhere in Scripture we learn that it was Israel's wisdom in using the law that was to become the envy of the other nations of the world (Deut. 4:5–8). Wisdom enables men and women to get things done, to use the skills that God has given them, and to enjoy the good gifts of this life properly. It takes time to get wisdom because wisdom requires a combination of knowledge and experience in both God's Word and his world, which results in skill.

We are not told exactly how the poor man saved the city, but we would guess that he spoke and that the proper people heard him. This may be confirmed by verse seventeen: "The words of the wise heard in quiet are better than the shouting of a ruler among fools." The book of Proverbs verifies time and again that wisdom involves knowing when to speak and how to speak in a community. This community emphasis is seen in that much of what follows now in this last section of Ecclesiastes has to do with wisdom and folly as it relates to ruling and being ruled, to governing and being governed. As has been mentioned already, this concentration on kings is of permanent theological value because the church reigns with Christ. The wisdom literature instructs us as sons of the king, as princes, how to live.

Wisdom, however, is not merely technical skill. We do not say that a man who has technical skill is wise. He may be able to fix your car or paint your house or program your computer—but that is not wisdom; it is skill. Human wisdom has great practical value (2:13–14; 7:11; 9:16–18; 10:2, 12) because it involves words spoken to others and is inherently relational. Nevertheless, having acknowledged the practicality of wisdom, Solomon goes on to warn that wisdom is not some secret key that magically puts men and women in complete control of their lives. How is that?

A wise man cannot control how his words will be received. Wisdom does not always insure personal success because the majority of people do not always appreciate wisdom. It is evident in the story Solomon tells that even though wisdom saves the city, no one seemed to remember the poor man who gave the sage advice. This ingratitude of the people of the city is yet one more example of what is uncontrollable and fickle in human life—vapor. Wise men are often not appreciated because they are appraised by foolish standards—by their possessions, power, or privilege, for example.

The problem is, as we all know, that in human *politics*—and remember that the art of governing a *polis*, a "city," applies not merely to the civil realm but also (perhaps especially) to the church—the last word regularly goes to the loudest. The one who has access to the microphones and cameras or to the other technologies of power wins the hearts and minds of the foolish multitude. Sadly, this is often true in the church as well. Yelling and pounding the pulpit seems to get people's attention more effectively than a word gently spoken.

In this fallen world, this world in which God has cursed humanity with death, there is always a fly in the ointment so that even wisdom is vulnerable and is often rendered useless by just a little folly. "Dead flies make the perfumer's ointment give off a stench; so a little folly outweighs wisdom and honor" (10:1).

This is a great analogy to what Solomon has just written, "Wisdom is better than weapons of war, but one sinner destroys much good" (9:18). An expensive item can be quickly rendered useless or spoiled by a small insect. Costly things are vulnerable to contamination by small, seemingly insignificant things. So even the weightiness of wisdom can be "outweighed" by little action. A single, seemingly small foolish act can do much damage to an otherwise wise man.

One of the many ironies of human existence, another feature that marks its vaporousness, is that wise men and women are always vulnerable to folly. And that folly, even though it may be just a smidgen, may jeopardize all of our wisdom. Just think about how you are able to dismiss an otherwise knowledgeable and competent person because of some quirky characteristic or some small offense he or she may have committed against you.

So I believe that Solomon strives here in these proverbs to counter the introduction of an erroneous extrapolation—that somehow the wise man is able, by exercising his wisdom, to avoid the pitfalls of life (the vaporousness of life) and confidently to exploit every situation to his own advantage. Wisdom is superior to folly, but its power is conditional, which makes it quite vulnerable. It is risky to be wise.

Wisdom's superiority and advantage are balanced by the vulnerability of the wise. While Solomon has established both, he follows by speaking highly of wisdom (10:2–3).

> A wise man's heart inclines him to the right,
> but a fool's heart to the left.
> Even when the fool walks on the road, he lacks sense,
> and he says to everyone that he is a fool.

Remember that the "right" is the position of power, strength, blessing, and glory (Gen. 48:14; Isa. 41:10). The word translated "fool" here means "dullard" and is a description of the fool's dullmindedness. He is dense. The word "fool" also occurs in 10:12 and 15. The statement that he "lacks sense" literally reads "his mind is lacking" (10:3). Verse two indicates that it is all a matter of the "heart"—not emotions or affections, but our core commitments and orientation.

A fool cannot even walk along the road without betraying his stupidity. He is a tragedy because he cannot even see it himself. Fools lose touch with reality. They don't even realize how stupid they are acting. Think of the boss who is oblivious to his own arrogance. Even when most everyone knows who the cartoon character Dilbert is, we still find overseers everywhere who are like Dilbert's boss without any awareness of it.

Solomon next returns to the issue he raised in Ecclesiastes 9:17: "If the anger of the ruler rises against you, do not leave your place, for calmness will lay great offenses to rest" (10:4). He thereby advises a young person training to be a counselor or ruler to stick with his duty and remain calm when someone over him gets irate and turns on him. Do not be too quick to rebel and leave (compare Ecclesiastes 8:2–4). Do not join in plots against those in authority over you because you discover a little foolishness in them. Even great offenses—this probably refers to the loud, angry attack of a leader—can be allayed with calmness. You can defuse a volatile situation with self-control and calm maturity. Here is the power of wisdom over against the folly of a powerful ruler (9:13–16).

The fact that wise men and women need to deal with the powerful because they are not powerful themselves leads to the great evil of role reversals (10:5–7): "There is an evil that I have seen under the sun, as it were an error proceeding from the ruler: folly is set in many high places, and the rich sit in a low place. I have seen slaves on horses, and princes walking on the ground like slaves."

Wise men and women do not always rule (remember the story of 9:13ff). The scenario illustrated by Solomon represents a calamity, an evil, a curse suffered by men under the sun, *hebel*. How this happens is not explained, but the point is that it is not good. Wisdom and wise men and women do not always rule in post-fall cultures. Of course, those who rule have the power to make sure that their press agents portray them as wise. Solomon's observations warn us that we should not be deceived into thinking that everyone who is acclaimed as wise is in fact wise.

Next Solomon points out the risks involved in wisdom's success.

> He who digs a pit will fall into it,
> and a serpent will bite him who breaks through a wall.
> He who quarries stones is hurt by them,
> and he who splits logs is endangered by them.
> If the iron is blunt, and one does not sharpen the edge,
> he must use more strength,
> but wisdom helps one to succeed. (10:8–10)

He calls up four examples of the hazards that attend our successful accomplishment of common tasks. An entire venture can fail because of a small oversight or a momentary lapse in concentration or maybe a small hazard that was not sufficiently guarded against. This undergirds Solomon's thesis (9:18; 10:1) that a small amount of folly can undo much wisdom. Finally, Solomon declares that wisdom as skill does indeed bring some *advantage* (9:10b; cf. 1:3).

In the next passage (10:11–15), the skillful words of the wise are contrasted with the senseless talk of the fool.

> If the serpent bites before it is charmed,
> there is no advantage to the charmer.
> The words of a wise man's mouth win him favor,
> but the lips of a fool consume him.
> The beginning of the words of his mouth is foolishness,
> and the end of his talk is evil madness.
> A fool multiplies words,
> though no man knows what is to be,
> and who can tell him what will be after him?
> The toil of a fool wearies him,
> for he does not know the way to the city.

Verse eleven is a parable that goes with what follows in verse twelve. The snake charmer is the fool who does not have the skill to tame his serpent before he starts using it. The result is that it will bring no "advantage" to him. The serpent is the tongue, as Psalm 140:3 reminds us: "They make their tongue sharp as a serpents, and under their lips is the venom of asps."

Solomon writes, "A fool multiplies words, though no man knows what is to be, and who can tell him what will be after him?" (10:14). This means either that the fool cannot see what he is bringing on himself by his babbling or that the major problem with the fool is that he thinks he can predict the future. He pretends—or he has deluded himself into thinking—that the world is predictable and that he can deal with it. Thus, he makes foolish, confident statements.

This second option is more in line with the thrust of what

Solomon has been writing. Remember this theme in Ecclesiastes—the wise man is precisely the one who confesses ignorance of the future and who trusts God. Even the wise man remains ignorant of the appropriate times for action because God has not given access to the details of his plans (3:1ff); even a wise man has no privileged knowledge of God's purposes and plans. It is impossible for men to make use of the way in which the world has been organized, because God has deliberately withheld the knowledge of it. God has deliberately kept man in ignorance of the things that he needs to know in order to live with absolute security and uninterrupted success (read Ecclesiastes 9:11). The wise man knows he is never in a position to stop trusting God (Eccl. 8:16, 17). The wise man admits he has no control, no leverage over God and his creation, and so does not make brash, stupid claims about what he is going to do and accomplish (8:7–8).

The fool, refusing to acknowledge the vaporous nature of life, insists on toil (10:15). In the context of verse fourteen, the fool's toil represents a certain kind of activity. What the fool does here is *talk*; it's his *speaking* that wearies him. His ignorance about going to the city is probably a reference to his sinful refusal to submit to the wisdom of the community. He prefers to do things alone. Not knowing to go to the city means not knowing that he should seek counsel and advice.

The basic application here is simple: think before you speak and get counsel from those who loyally advise you before displaying your wisdom to the world.

Of course, as we have seen, wisdom rarely gives us sayings that do not require qualification, and this is no exception. Even though it is foolish not to know the way to the city, the city can itself also be a place of foolishness. Solomon now addresses that possibility, pointing out that even rulers who live in the city can be so foolish as to not really know the way to the city.

> Woe to you, O land, when your king is a child,
> and your princes feast in the morning!
> Happy are you, O land, when your king is the son of the nobility,

> and your princes feast at the proper time,
> for strength, and not for drunkenness!
> Through sloth the roof sinks in,
> and through indolence the house leaks.
> Bread is made for laughter,
> and wine gladdens life,
> and money answers everything.
> Even in your thought, do not curse the king,
> nor in your bedroom curse the rich,
> for a bird of the air will carry your voice,
> or some winged creature tell the matter. (10:16–20)

Children live hand-to-mouth. If they were permitted to have their way they would eat snacks and candy all day and watch movies all night. Thus, rulers who are so immature as to act this way will ruin a land. A wise ruler knows when to work and when to feast. The wise balance of these activities makes for a strong house. If a man has refused to grow up, he will be a drain on a kingdom rather than an asset as a ruler (c.f. Isaiah 3:1–12; 5:11ff; 28:7ff; Amos 6:4ff).

The ESV makes Solomon's point more difficult to understand by translating the last clause of verse nineteen as "money answers everything." The verse simply means "to provide for." If you are going to feast and find happiness and joy in your household, then you will have to have the means (money) to provide for it. Solomon is reinforcing his point that sloth will cause poverty (10:18) and that one must be moderate rather than profligate in enjoying good things (10:17). The stress here is on moderation, balance, and appropriateness. The wise ruler will see the need to practice these things and will have the self-control to do so.

Solomon has told us to enjoy life, to embrace wine, wife, and song, but at the same time he has told us to enjoy our work. Obviously, none of his exhortations for us to enjoy wine, food, and other things are meant to be taken as directions to do nothing else. One must wisely know when it is appropriate to work and to play. So here Solomon points out that the house will collapse if one does not restrain oneself (10:18). Here, the "house" may be the political structure of the land, but it would also apply to each domestic household and how the rulers in that house must act wisely.

Though it is great to see what wise rulers should be like, what about wise subjects under a foolish ruler? It is all too easy to think one is wise simply because one recognizes the foolishness of one's ruler, but that can simply be a form of boastful arrogance, an attempt to raise oneself by bettering those who are in power. Most people *think* they can do better than whoever is over them and they often delight to tell others that it is so. A wise person is not wise according to what he *does* say or think about those in power, but rather (and more importantly) according to what he *does not* say.

Even in extreme circumstances one should be careful not to curse those in authority. Even one's most secret thoughts and intimate words have a way of becoming known—primarily because we can all be such fools with the way we reveal our thoughts. The Law taught, "You shall not revile God, nor curse a ruler of your people" (Ex. 22:28; cf. Rom. 13:2; Titus 3:1). Solomon in his wisdom points out that it would be wise to give *anyone* with power over you that sort of deference, not only "the king," but simply "the rich."

Solomon here is coming full circle, returning to the theme of 9:17 and 10:4—that small lapses in judgment can have great consequences. A little foolishness, especially rash rebellion and insubordination, have a way of becoming public. Remember the vulnerability of both wisdom and one's position. Even the wise man's life is forever at risk since it can be undermined at any time by indiscretion. In verse twenty it is a bird, just as in verses eight through eleven it is a snake or a rock or a splinter from a log. In verse one, it is merely a fly. All are small and apparently insignificant creatures and things. Foolishness is like that. It always threatens the wise man or woman.

This section has moved from the power of wisdom to the reality of its vulnerability. One of the follies it is easy for a wise man to fall into is to imagine that his wisdom somehow renders him powerful and protected. Wisdom's power to protect, such as it is, lies precisely in acknowledging one's limitations and vulnerabilities.

11

Bread Upon the Waters: Ecclesiastes 11:1–6

Give, and it will be given to you. A good measure, pressed down, shaken together, running over, will be put into your lap. For with the measure you use it will be measured back to you. —Luke 6:38

I had the opportunity to think about this passage one day while I was cutting the grass. My two little ones were out with me in the yard and wanted something to do. Since this passage was on my mind, I thought about it when I gave the pruning shears to my daughter and then to my younger son to cut some huge weeds that had grown up here and there next to the house. I said to them, "Be careful! Watch your fingers. Cut the weeds, not your fingers." There is a moment of anxiety that comes over a parent when he lets his children take risks. Think of what could happen! But you've got to give them opportunities to learn and grow. They must grow up.

Right?

> Cast your bread upon the waters,
> for you will find it after many days.
> Give a portion to seven, or even to eight,
> for you know not what disaster may happen on earth.
> If the clouds are full of rain,
> they empty themselves on the earth,
> and if a tree falls to the south or to the north,
> in the place where the tree falls, there it will lie.
> He who observes the wind will not sow,
> and he who regards the clouds will not reap.
>
> As you do not know the way the spirit comes to the bones in the womb of a woman with child, so you do not know the work of God who makes everything.
>
> In the morning sow your seed, and at evening withhold not your hand, for you do not know which will prosper, this or that, or whether both alike will be good. (11:1–6)

This passage is about taking risks. It is about the temptations that arise in this uncertain, uncontrollable world. Will we just do nothing? The note of caution sounded in chapter 10 cannot be allowed to paralyze us. Oh my, there will be flies in the ointment! We should stop making it! Our disorientation and fear stemming from wisdom's vulnerability must not be allowed drive us to paralyzing anxiety or the crippling inactivity of despair.

Time and events overtake everyone (9:11) and you have no ultimate control over the outcome of your ventures. This fact forces you to confront a basic choice. Since there are risks involved in every activity under the sun, either you can pull back and take the least amount of risks for fear of future calamity—hoard and hug all the resources you have to yourself—or you can allow this knowledge to free you up for enterprising activity. The vaporous nature of life may lead to despairing inactivity or faithful fullness of life. Which will it be? We have already heard the verdict as to how we ought to act: embrace the fullness of life, joy, and happiness. There is nothing better for a man to do!

What is that fullness of life that Solomon urges us toward? What does it look like? How does *faith* live in this vaporous life under the sun, in this life in which we cannot—by all our investigating, thinking, or working—lever the world to work in our favor? How then shall we live? Solomon brings us to the conclusion of the matter in 11:1 through 12:8. The evangelical commentator Derek Kidner summarizes it well. Be bold (11:1–6) or better, be generous! Be joyful (11:7–10). Be godly (12:1–8).

To understand verses one through six we need to see them as the answer to a riddle that Solomon has been asking over and over again. We know that Solomon has encouraged us to "do good" (3:12), but he has not been forthcoming with exactly how we are to do good. What specifically does he want us to do? And what is the "labor," this "work" to which Solomon has been cryptically referring all along in the conclusions to his various sections of Ecclesiastes? Remember, he was searching for what was most beneficial for man to do. "I searched with my heart how to cheer my body with wine—my heart still guiding me with wisdom—and how to lay hold on folly, till I might see what was *good* for the children of man *to do* under heaven during the few days of their life" (2:3, emphasis added).

Who is this "one who pleases . . . God" in 2:26, to whom God gives wisdom, knowledge, and joy? We received a strong hint from Solomon in chapter 4. The one who does good is the one who shares his life with another and who has another with whom to share:

> Again, I saw [vapor] under the sun: one person who has no other, either son or brother, yet there is no end to all his toil, and his eyes are never satisfied with riches, so that he never asks, "For whom am I toiling and depriving myself of pleasure?" This also is [vapor] and a miserable business.
>
> Two are better than one, because they have a good reward for their toil. For if they fall, one will lift up his fellow. But woe to him who is alone when he falls and has not another to lift him up! Again, if two lie together, they keep warm, but how can one keep warm alone? And though a man might prevail against one who is alone, two will withstand him—a threefold cord is not quickly broken. (4:7–12).

Now Solomon makes it *relatively* plain (it's still couched language that only the wise will be able to discern). The lesson of the first six verses of chapter 11 is foundational. Despite life's vaporous uncontrollability and even wisdom's vulnerability, the Creator promises ultimate fulfillment when his people trust him and venture to serve others. Thus, Solomon exhorts us to be generous (1–2a).

Some have argued for other interpretations, but the last clause exhorting us to give a portion to seven or eight seems rather clear, and interprets the parable of casting bread. An interpretation involving a call for commercial investment may be a factor. In that case "bread upon the waters" is more or less equivalent to money sent overseas. Is Solomon advocating the risky business of overseas trade? This option would not exclude the possibility that Solomon is calling on us to share with others. Thus the ancient proverb: "Whoso giveth alms is like a merchant who sends his property overseas."

It will help us to remember that during Solomon's reign, a great deal of "*bread*" came back to him over the waters. When Solomon ruled as king, Israel came as close as she ever did to fulfilling her divine calling to be a kingdom of priests ministering to and serving the world. Israel was chosen not to exclude everyone else, but to bring blessing to all the families of the earth (Gen. 12:1–3). This meant Israel's stance needed to be outward-facing. This happened rarely, if at all, before the period of wisdom and kings. With Solomon we begin to see Israel taking up her calling. We need to recall Solomon's relationship with the nations.

> Now Hiram king of Tyre sent his servants to Solomon when he heard that they had anointed him king in place of his father, for Hiram always loved David. And Solomon sent word to Hiram, "You know that David my father could not build a house for the name of the Lord his God because of the warfare with which his enemies surrounded him, until the Lord put them under the soles of his feet. But now the Lord my God has given me rest on every side. There is neither adversary nor misfortune. And so I intend to build a house for the name of the Lord my God, as the Lord said to David my father, 'Your son, whom I will set on your throne in your place, shall build the house for my name.' Now therefore com-

> mand that cedars of Lebanon be cut for me. And my servants will join your servants, and I will pay you for your servants such wages as you set, for you know that there is no one among us who knows how to cut timber like the Sidonians."
>
> As soon as Hiram heard the words of Solomon, he rejoiced greatly and said, "Blessed be the Lord this day, who has given to David a wise son to be over this great people." And Hiram sent to Solomon, saying, "I have heard the message that you have sent to me. I am ready to do all you desire in the matter of cedar and cypress timber. My servants shall bring it down to the sea from Lebanon, and I will make it into rafts to go by sea to the place you direct. And I will have them broken up there, and you shall receive it. And you shall meet my wishes by providing food for my household." So Hiram supplied Solomon with all the timber of cedar and cypress that he desired, while Solomon gave Hiram 20,000 cors of wheat as food for his household, and 20,000 cors of beaten oil. Solomon gave this to Hiram year by year. And the Lord gave Solomon wisdom, as he promised him. And there was peace between Hiram and Solomon, and the two of them made a treaty. (1 Kings 5:1–12)

As a result of this relationship, Solomon's vessels returned from Tarshish once every three years, bringing with them rich cargoes. "For the king had a fleet of ships of Tarshish at sea with the fleet of Hiram. Once every three years the fleet of ships of Tarshish used to come bringing gold, silver, ivory, apes, and peacocks" (1 Kings 10:22). Dealing with the nations and ministering to them had great rewards.

Of course, throwing bread onto water does not appear to be a rational form of investment! Solomon is issuing a call to be boldly generous and lavishly good to our neighbors. This is the epitome of wisdom even though it looks like a losing proposition. Wisdom does not walk by sight but by faith. "Whoever is generous to the poor lends to Yahweh, and he will repay him for his deed" (Prov. 19:17). It comes down to whether or not we trust God to keep his word. We cannot control life and *make* our generosity come back to us, but God is faithful. Thus, when we look at the description of Lady Wisdom at the end of Proverbs (31:10ff), we find she is provident, entrepreneurial, and known for her generosity to those who have needs.

As the true wise King, Jesus backs up what Solomon tells us: "Give to everyone who begs from you, and from one who takes away your goods do not demand them back . . . give, and it will be given to you. Good measure, pressed down, shaken together, running over, will be put into your lap. For with the measure you use it will be measured back to you" (Luke 6:30, 38). To follow Jesus requires *faith* in God's integrity and ability to keep his promises. This ethic of faith was passed on from Jesus into the New Testament church:

> The point is this: whoever sows sparingly will also reap sparingly, and whoever sows bountifully will also reap bountifully. Each one must give as he has made up his mind, not reluctantly or under compulsion, for God loves a cheerful giver. And God is able to make all grace abound to you, so that having all sufficiency in all things at all times, you may abound in every good work. As it is written,
>
> > "He has distributed freely, he has given to the poor;
> > his righteousness endures forever."
>
> He who supplies seed to the sower and bread for food will supply and multiply your seed for sowing and increase the harvest of your righteousness. (2 Cor. 9:6–10)

> And you Philippians yourselves know that in the beginning of the gospel, when I left Macedonia, no church entered into partnership with me in giving and receiving, except you only. Even in Thessalonica you sent me help for my needs once and again. Not that I seek the gift, but I seek the fruit that increases to your credit. I have received full payment, and more. I am well supplied, having received from Epaphroditus the gifts you sent, a fragrant offering, a sacrifice acceptable and pleasing to God. *And my God will supply every need of yours according to his riches in glory in Christ Jesus.* (Phil. 4:15–19, emphasis added)

The basis for Christian charity is not simply love, but also a proper confidence. God gives of himself generously. In a sense, the way he does so is unique. God is all-sufficient so that he can be the ever-giving God (Jas. 1:5). We might infer from God's uniqueness that there is no way we can use him as a model for our own behavior. We, after all, are not infinite, nor self-sustaining. The reason why God's generosity remains a model for us, despite this great difference, is precisely because we can trust God to bring our bread back to us. We are supplied by his abundance. It all comes down to faith. We can be extravagant in our generosity as well precisely because God is faithful and abundantly generous.

In keeping with this principle, Solomon exhorts us to "give a portion to seven, or even to eight" (11:2a), as if to say the number seven does not mark the limit of the extent of our benevolence. Give to the utmost—seven; but even beyond seven, to eight! We are to be rivers of generosity. "He has distributed freely; he has given to the poor; his righteousness endures forever; his horn is exalted in honor" (Ps. 112:9).

What are we doing as Christians to "cast our bread upon the waters," to give out portions to seven and eight? Perhaps we do not do more because we are waiting to be in a position to be better able to afford to give to others. While there are certain instances where Christians must use caution, in general, the desire to wait until one is better off before reaching out is nothing more than another attempt to control the wind. It is vapor; and Solomon goes on (11:2b–4) to warn us against thinking that tomorrow will be a better day for outreach, concluding, "He who observes the wind will not sow, and he who regards the clouds will not reap" (Eccl. 11:4).

Clouds and trees follow their own laws and times, not ours; or better, they follow God's laws and times. And this is not available to us. We can do nothing about the time and place that rain falls. A tree does not consult your convenience before it falls this way or that. It just does what it does. Clouds, along with wind and rain, remember, are often images of judgment and designations of trouble or evil (Eccl. 12:2).

Solomon's point is simple: if you spend too much time watching the wind to see which way the tree is going to fall, or gazing up at the sky wringing your hands waiting for the ideal weather conditions before you plant, then it is more likely that you will never take the risk that you need to take in order to begin. Will the conditions ever be ideal? We will wait around and never get anything done if we think that conditions have to be ideal before we move out and take the risks of giving and investing. We are tempted to hoard if we think that a disaster or a calamity is on the horizon. Solomon warns us against that covetous narrow-heartedness, which, in times of distress, so easily creeps into our hearts.

Perhaps some of you had Christian friends who, in 1999, were afraid that the so-called "Y2K Bug" would end western civilization. I had parishioners coming to me asking my advice. I found in virtually every case that they were being told to become survivalists in the name of Jesus, and that they should acquire isolated property, hoard gold, guns, and groceries, and provide only for themselves.

In the case of one wealthy Christian, I asked him what he should do *as a Christian*. He said that he thought that such a disaster would be an opportunity to serve friends and neighbors who need help. Precisely. "How can you do that if you've isolated your family in some compound in the Ozark Mountains?" I asked. Well, this particular man said that surviving in itself would be a service to future generations. "Yes," I said, "it's always easy to serve people that don't exist. Besides, I think the best way to serve them would be to leave them an example of self-effacing love and mercy in the midst of the crisis. If these dire predictions actually come true then the church cannot pull out and hide in the woods! We've got to be in the heart of the suffering and pain ministering the love and compassion of Christ to our neighbors and friends."

It was the Christians who held civilization together in the Middle Ages during plagues and crises. They stayed in the cities. The rest of the population split. With disasters like Hurricane Katrina, it is important for us to think this through and commit ourselves to real trust in God. I am all for adjusting your personal investment portfolio in order to provide for your family. And if you want to store food and stuff at your home, fine, but do not run off with it when the crisis begins. Stay in your neighborhood and pass it out.

In order to understand what Solomon goes on to say in verse

five, it might be helpful to see how faithful Hebrews later in history may have applied it. We have an example in the story recorded for us in the ancient book of 2 Maccabees 7. While this story is quite possibly (or even probably) fictional or at least fictionalized, it does show us how ancient Jews two-thousand-plus years ago took the formation of a child in the womb as a sign to hope in God.

In this story, seven brothers and their mother are tortured to death because they refuse to eat the meat of a pig, since pig is an unclean animal according to the Mosaic Law and is forbidden to Jews. While the first brother is mutilated and then fried to death in a big pan, his mother and brothers "encouraged one another to die nobly, saying, 'The Lord God is watching over us and in truth has compassion on us, as Moses declared in his song which bore witness against the people to their faces when he said, "And he will have compassion on his servants" ' " (2 Macc. 7:5b–6). Though their mother is forced to watch the successive gruesome murders of her children one after another, she encourages them, saying, "I do not know how you came into being in my womb. It was not I who gave you life and breath, nor I who set in order the elements within each of you. Therefore the Creator of the world, who shaped the beginning of man and devised the origin of all things, will in his mercy give life and breath back to you again, since you now forget yourselves for the sake of his laws" (2 Macc. 7:23–24).

Instead of killing the last brother right away, the pagan king offered him life and wealth and power if he would eat pork. He ordered the victim's mother to persuade her son to accept his offer. Instead the woman said to her son in Hebrew, "My son, have pity on me. I carried you nine months in my womb, and nursed you for three years, and have reared you and brought you up to this point in your life, and have taken care of you. I beseech you, my child, to look at the heaven and the earth and see everything that is in them, and recognize that God did not make them out of things that existed. Thus also mankind comes into being. Do not fear this butcher. Accept death, so that in God's mercy I may get you back again with your brothers" (2 Macc. 7:27b–29).

It is noteworthy that the narrator explains the mother's courage as being caused by "her hope in the Lord" (v. 20). Likewise, when the seventh son willingly went to his death, it was the result of "putting his whole trust in the Lord" (v. 39).

We do not know how God makes life in the womb and gives the breath of life to babies. This mother took that as a sign that even though they didn't understand how resurrection is possible, God must be able to do it and he could be trusted. She and her sons were called to the ultimate act of casting bread upon the water, not knowing how it could come back to them, but trusting God that he would bring it back to them. He would raise them from the dead, giving them back the parts of their body that were severed from them and burned up.

Solomon is pointing out that fear makes no sense. Waiting for the point when the future will become predictable and risk-free means never casting one's bread upon the waters. The work of the Spirit in making new life is hidden from us. How God will provide for us will not be visible to us.

The "way of the spirit" here could refer to a child's own life. Indeed, the word for spirit could be translated differently so it refers to the "way of the breath" of life, but the phrase could also refer to the Giver of Life: "the way of the Spirit." Solomon is probably making a double entendre. Whatever the case, notice how it seems Jesus was using this passage when he spoke to Nicodemus: "The wind blows where it wishes, and you hear its sound, but you do not know where it comes from or where it goes. So it is with everyone who is born of the Spirit" (John 3:8).

Even if we cannot be sure how we will succeed, surely we should be generous and openhanded. This idea of success, profit, or advantage is a key one, you will remember, in Ecclesiastes. It goes all the way back to the programmatic question of 1:3. Even though our toil is intrinsically nothing more than vapor, God himself causes our work to prosper and profit. The Spirit's hidden work is a function of God the Creator's freedom, all of which means that you and I cannot understand the work of God. It is beyond our comprehension and control. It is *vapor* to try to figure it out. Do what God commands and leave the results to him.

Truly, our knowledge is severely limited, but we are fools if we permit this ignorance to reduce us to impotence. The process and the end product are not within our power to know or control. One is reminded of Jesus's parable, "The kingdom of God is as if a man should scatter seed on the ground. He sleeps and rises night and day, and the seed sprouts and grows; he knows not how. The earth produces by itself, first the blade, then the ear, then the full grain in the ear" (Mark 4:26–28). And so Solomon advises, "In the morning sow your seed, and at evening withhold not your hand, for you do not know which will prosper, this or that, or whether both alike will be good" (11:6). This is the proper response to the *hebelness* of life—redouble your efforts. Be incessantly active, day and night. "The point is this: whoever sows sparingly will also reap sparingly, and he who sows bountifully will also reap bountifully" (2 Cor. 9:6).

Far from encouraging slothfulness, vapor is a motivation. Our own ignorance, lack of control, and the likelihood of calamity are all reasons for a wise person to redouble his or her efforts. Wisdom works! A wise man gives and distributes and serves, leaving the outcome in God's hands.

This comes to fulfillment in the gospel accounts. Jesus Christ is the man who alone lived this life of pure generosity. He was the one who trusted his Father for the outcome. He was the one who was moved by the Spirit, who was given to him without measure. And by the Spirit he gave himself for us all! And that same Spirit, who formed him in his mother's womb, also remade him by raising him from the dead (Rom. 1:2; 8:11).

Did Jesus know exactly *how* everything was going to turn out? Was he fully human? Fully subject to the vaporousness of life as we are? Yes. Did he wrestle with his Father in the garden of Gethsemane questioning, imploring, anxious about "casting his bread upon the waters"—that bread of life, his body, which he *gave* as life for the world? Again, yes. Was it easy for him? Did he not have to trust his Father and faithfully give of himself? *Of course he did*! Was he vindicated? Did the seed planted in the ground bear much fruit?

Yes; and so we have a firm basis for our faith in the God who raised Jesus from the dead.

Solomon's wisdom was embodied in Jesus, the Anointed One, the greater and final Son of David. This is no longer for us merely wise and godly advice. It has been confirmed and is as sure as Jesus's resurrection by the Spirit from the dead. That is why the New Testament depicts Jesus's disciples following him in the same kind of self-denying life of generous giving. If Jesus has given his life as bread to feed the world, then we too should become living sacrifices and be broken and distributed as bread to a hungry world. This is true in church and in any healthy and free Christian culture, and it is also true in the marketplace and the neighborhood.

12

The Conclusion of the Matter: Ecclesiastes 11:7–12:14

One becomes a theologian not by understanding, reading, and speculating, but by living, dying, and being damned.
—Martin Luther, Commentary on the Psalms

It is not uncommon for children to hate the idea that their parents are intimate with one another. This goes beyond the simple appropriate limits we should all adhere to in what we think about. Sons or daughters react almost physically with disgust at the thought of their parents acting the same way they want and expect to act when they are married. Somehow, the imprint of their parents as caregivers seems to exclude the possibility that they are romantically and sexually involved. It just seems wrong somehow.

I wonder if we have been imprinted with an idea of how the Bible is supposed to "behave" that leaves us, sometimes, quite uncomfortable with what it actually says and teaches. Does the Bible seem to address areas that we don't think it should address because it is a "religious" book? Does it touch upon matters that we have somehow trained ourselves to feel are inappropriate for such a holy book?

In our church we often sing a hymn called the Lorica, especially when there is a baptism. It is a version of a song known also as "Saint Patrick's Breastplate." The fourth stanza makes some striking claims:

> I bind unto myself today
> the virtues of the starlit heav'n,
> the glorious sun's life-giving ray,
> the whiteness of the moon at even,
> the flashing of the lightning free,
> the whirling winds tempestuous shocks,
> the stable earth, the deep salt sea
> around the old undying rocks.

I wonder how many in the congregation, when they first sung these words, felt like there was something wrong with these verses. At least when they first begin singing it, I imagine many do find it odd. In the middle of singing about baptism into the Triune name, suddenly we are singing of stars and lightning, ocean and rocks. It seems like Christian worship is going into an inappropriate area of life. Why sing about nature at this point?

This cannot stand up to any sort of biblical scrutiny. The hymn is nothing more than an expression of full-bodied Christian faith. When God reintegrates us into his life, he also reintegrates us into his creation. He connects us to it rightly. As the apostle Paul wrote, "So let no one boast in men. For all things are yours, whether Paul or Apollos or Cephas or the world or life or death or the present or the future—all are yours, and you are Christ's, and Christ is God's" (1 Cor. 3:21–23). Jesus is not simply the Savior of one's individual soul. Even if you add your body to the mix and look for bodily transformation at the resurrection, that is not enough. He is not plucking us out of our material environment. Rather, he is the Savior and Reconciler of all creation. As Paul assures us, Jesus is

> the head of the body, the church. He is the beginning, the firstborn from the dead, that *in everything* He might be preeminent. For in Him all the fullness of God was pleased to dwell, and through Him to reconcile to Himself *all things, whether on earth or in heaven*, making peace by the blood of His cross. And you, who once were alienated and hostile in mind, doing evil deeds, He has now reconciled in His body of flesh by His death, in order to present you holy and blameless and above reproach before Him, if indeed you continue in the faith, stable and steadfast, not shifting from the hope of the gospel that you heard, *which has been proclaimed in all creation under heaven*. (Col. 1:18–23)

We need to stop compartmentalizing the world. God's covenant with us is his covenant in Christ with all creation. In this biblical context, one shouldn't even raise an eyebrow that Solomon sings the praises of work, wife, feasting, and drinking wine. If that seems too physical, worldly, or unspiritual, maybe it is time for us to get a grip on what the Bible says is truly spiritual.

In a sense, Ecclesiastes is a doubly-condemned book by the standards of American piety. On the one hand, Solomon gets in trouble with us for looking unflinchingly at the evil in the world—at injustice, death, disaster, tyranny, the futility of man's work, the uncontrollable future. We want to pretend there is a much rosier reality available to us, but this is—to call a spade a spade—unbelief. The world is what it is, not what we would like it to be. And, more to the point, the world is what it is because God made it that way. Deceiving ourselves does not show much faith in God. Self-deception never does. On the other hand, in the face of all this wind-shepherding folly, Solomon embraces and affirms life as a gift from God and exhorts us to embrace and affirm life by truly enjoying it. Solomon's life-affirming statements also cut across the grain of common Christian piety.

The common thread here is escapism. We seek to escape both the problems of this world by denying their reality and escape the pleasures of life by denying their propriety, but the biblical religion is *not* escapist. The grace of God trains us "to renounce ungodliness and worldly passion" (Titus 2:11–12), not to renounce the good things God gives us. On the contrary, these things are to be received *with thanks* (1 Tim. 4:3).

Thus we now see that Solomon continues his series of bold imperatives. In chapter 10 he told us to *be wise* and in 11:1–6 he told us to *be generous*. Then he told us to *be joyful* (11:7–10), and now we are summoned to *be godly* (12:1–8). And all of this without any sense that these three concerns are in tension with one another. His two last exhortations are marked in verse eight of chapter 11 by his twin commands to "rejoice" and "remember." He emphasizes these two commands with his refrain about vapor. "Vapor," then, ends the two sections (11:7–10; 12:1–8), reminding the reader of the thematic commands in verse eight.

> Light is sweet, and it is pleasant for the eyes to see the sun.
>
> So if a person lives many years, let him rejoice in them all; but let him remember that the days of darkness will be many. All that comes is [vapor].
>
> Rejoice, O young man, in your youth, and let your heart cheer you in the days of your youth. Walk in the ways of your heart and the sight of your eyes. But know that for all these things God will bring you into judgment. Remove vexation from your heart, and put away pain from your body, for youth and the dawn of life are [vapor]. (11:7–10)

Once again, the wise shepherd king commends *joy*. Continually, Solomon teaches us that wisdom means joy. This has come through loud and clear in Ecclesiastes, especially every time he reaches a partial conclusion. And now again, as he draws near to the end of his work, without sacrificing his realism, Solomon affirms life in all its fullness, beginning with "light" as a metaphor (11:7–8). However many years a man may have of life, let him enjoy them all.

Flowing from 11:1–6, there really is a sense in which we can be, as Christians, a little light-hearted about life. If we truly confess and believe that God is in control of his world, then for us, everything to come is vapor (11:8c). It is all in God's hands, as Solomon has said over and over again. And so I often tell those who are over-anxious about everything, "Relax. Have some chips and dip. The Lord is in control of it all."

Specifically in this section, your future life, the length of your days, your age at your death, the success of your labors, are all aspects of the future that remain outside of your knowledge and control. *So be happy while you are young* (11:9). This youthful radiance commended to us by Solomon may indeed continue to the end of your life ("if a person lives many years, let him rejoice in them all," 11:8a). The adjective "young" here is used in a relative sense. Anyone who has not reached the state of 12:2–5 just before death is young. Even if our light-filled life is punctuated often with times of darkness—"let him remember that the days of darkness will be many. All that comes is vapor"—we should learn our lesson from these times, that the future is vapor to us. We cannot hope to control it.

Again, Solomon refuses to see life as a choice between despair and delusion. There is no need to ignore these times of darkness, to pretend that they do not exist! Solomon's wisdom says that you either face the facts (11:8b) or they will overwhelm you (11:10a).

There is a widespread mistaken notion that biblical faith stifles and chokes any kind of freedom of thought and living. But Solomon is quite explicit, especially in 11:9: enjoy the years that God gives you, take advantage of your youth, and, most shocking of all, follow your heart! This almost sounds like a passage from the literature of the Romantic period in America. Perhaps we need to insist that biblical religion is the true romanticism. Yet this is not the only place where "follow your heart" is seen as a pious statement. 11:9a is akin to the saying found elsewhere in the Old Testament, "Do all that is in your heart" (1 Sam. 14:7). The overarching point in the Bible is that, while some things are prohibited, everything else is left wide open for you to pursue if your heart so desires.

The judgment spoken of at the end of this verse (11:9b) is not meant to kill the joy and happiness of life. Solomon does not hang this sword over us so as to squelch our joy. The point is that our ways actually matter to God. Life is *not* meaningless or vanity. He knows them all. Awareness of God's evaluation both helps us fear to do evil, and it gives us confidence in doing good by faith (Gal. 6:9).

In verse ten, Solomon explicitly addresses what you need to do in order to rejoice: set yourself free from worry. You do not control the future. Youth and health and life and vigor are not yours to control. They are vapor. God controls them.

This word variously translated "worry" or "anxiety" or "vexation" (KJV; ESV) has been used throughout the book. It refers to a bitterness provoked by the harsh realities of life under the sun. It is the fool's response to the *hebelness* of life (see 7:9). The fool has not rightly discerned his own vaporous existence. He is frustrated because he cannot manipulate existence to serve him. He has not "put away calamity [ESV, 'evil'] from his flesh, for youth and vigor are vapor." Consider Jesus's own development of this principle:

> Therefore I tell you, do not be anxious about your life, what you will eat or what you will drink, nor about your body, what you will put on. Is not life more than food, and the body more than clothing? Look at the birds of the air: they neither sow nor reap nor gather into barns, and yet your heavenly Father feeds them. Are you not of more value than they? And which of you by being anxious can add a single hour to his span of life? And why are you anxious about clothing? Consider the lilies of the field, how they grow: they neither toil nor spin, yet I tell you, even Solomon in all his glory was not arrayed like one of these. But if God so clothes the grass of the field, which today is alive and tomorrow is thrown into the oven, will He not much more clothe you, O you of little faith? Therefore do not be anxious, saying, "What shall we eat?" or "What shall we drink?" or "What shall we wear?" For the Gentiles seek after all these things, and your heavenly Father knows that you need them all. But seek first the kingdom of God and His righteousness, and all these things will be added to you. Therefore do not be anxious about tomorrow, for tomorrow will be anxious for itself. Sufficient for the day is its own trouble.

Be joyful, *but also be godly.* Solomon returns in 12:1–8 to the name that he has used to describe God in this book—the *Creator* or *Maker* of all things (12:1; 11:5). This Creator, remember, is the one who, according to chapter 3, has made everything fitting in its time. He sets the pattern of our existence as a whole. He will call the past to account (3:15). Specifically, the creator is the one who has given you life and every good thing.

> Remember also your Creator in the days of your youth, before the evil days come and the years draw near of which you will say, "I have no pleasure in them"; before the sun and the light and the moon and the stars are darkened and the clouds return after the rain, in the day when the keepers of the house tremble, and the strong men are bent, and the grinders cease because they are few, and those who look through the windows are dimmed, and the doors on the street are shut—when the sound of the grinding is low, and one rises up at the sound of a bird, and all the daughters of song are brought low—they are afraid also of what is high, and terrors are in the way; the almond tree blossoms, the grasshopper drags itself along, and desire fails, because man is going to his eternal home, and the mourners go about the streets—before the silver cord is snapped, or the golden bowl is broken, or the pitcher is shattered at the fountain, or the wheel broken at the cistern, and the dust returns to the earth as it was, and the spirit returns to God who gave it. [Vapor] of [vapors], says the Preacher; all is [vapor]. (12:1–8)

Here "remembering" is not so much contrasted with forgetting, but with the loss of pleasure in life that will come with age. The exhortation to remember your Creator is an exhortation to remember his gifts and take pleasure (12:12c) in their use while you still can. All things are yours, but one day you will no longer be able to enjoy them.

It is the fact of death that must be remembered, that is, faced squarely and honestly. It is death that manifests the ultimate vapor-character of life. The wise man knows this much (9:1–6; 7:2; 9:11). There's no escaping death, and in a genuinely biblical view of life, death cannot be minimized or avoided.

Solomon emphasizes this with a poem (12:1b–5) and the poetry, like all good poetry, needs to be felt and not necessarily overanalyzed. It is a somber, realistic portrayal of the darkening years of old age and approaching death. We encounter a succession of images of distortion and despair: trembling, writhing, cessation of activity, darkening, shutting, silence, bowing, and fear. As someone wisely observed, "In one's early years, and for the greater part of life, troubles and illnesses are chiefly set-backs, not disasters. One expects the sky to clear eventually. It is hard to adjust to the closing of that long chapter: to know that now, in the final stretch, there will be no improvement: the clouds will always gather again, and time will no longer heal, but kill."

It is best that we reflect upon these realities when we are young so that there will be fewer regrets and fewer missed opportunities. As the saying goes, youth is wasted on the young. Wisdom helps us avoid later lamenting the times we were given but did not receive with thankfulness.

Solomon's poem gives us a succession of images. Verse two presents us with the metaphor of nightfall, storm, and winter. Then in 12:3–4a, we are shown a great house in decline. The house and its inhabitants lose their glory and power. The image shifts in verse four to suggest an old man who can no longer be roused in the morning by the sound of birds. With old age, these cheerful evidences of a living world about us grow faint and remote. Verse five continues a portrait of an old man's frailties. The almond tree is probably a reference to white hair. The grasshopper dragging is used as a parody of the old man's slow, stiff walk. Grasshoppers are made to jump and spring from place to place, but when one is dying all it can do is drag itself along. One is reminded of the confession of an aged man in Scripture, "I am this day eighty years old. Can I discern what is pleasant and what is not? Can your servant taste what he eats or what he drinks? Can I still listen to the voice of singing men and singing women?" (2 Sam. 19:35a).

Solomon stops using metaphors (12:5b) and speaks of a funeral before reverting back to poetry. In verse six he uses three metaphors for death. First he writes of a lamp that has been shattered, lost its oil, and no longer burns: "the lamp . . . goes out" (Prov. 13:9; Zech. 4:3). In Solomon's imagery life is like a golden lamp suspended by a silver chain. If one link fails the whole thing will break and come crashing down. Not only is the light of the lamp gone but the oil is spilled because the bowl is broken. Second, the pitcher is shattered at the well so that it can no longer hold the water. Finally, life is compared to a wheel. Since this wheel is at a cistern, it designates a pulley that is broken and useless for retrieving water.

Man, in short (12:7), is like an earthen vessel. When he comes to an end the vessel returns to the ground from which it came and its contents flow away. The days Solomon describes (12:2–7) will unquestionably come upon us all. For most of us they have come or will come to our grandparents and parents first, and then to us. No one escapes and no one can do anything about it. Death, and therefore life, is outside our control. It is all *vapor* (12:8).

To recap at the end of Ecclesiastes what I have pointed out from the beginning, the notion that *hebel* means "vanity" and is a catchword for a pessimistic, humanistic view of life as meaningless is severely mistaken. Solomon has instructed us in the enigmatic and uncontrollable character of our lives and the events that shape them. They are out of our control, but he has repeatedly urged us, nonetheless, to receive and enjoy life as a gift from God. Enjoy your life and world in all of its mystery.

It is amazingly ironic that often Christians will disparage the pleasures of life because they are "vanity." Solomon comes to exactly the opposite conclusion. Because our work and life are "vapor," we must enjoy these things while we have them. Do you like to read? The time is coming when you will not read anymore. Do you like sports? The time is coming when you can neither be a spectator nor an athlete. Do you love to cook? The time is coming when you won't be able to smell the food or take pleasure in preparing it. Disparaging such things now while you have them would be the mark of a fool. Once again, the conclusion is familiar. Be wise. Trust God and enjoy life.

Besides being wise, the Pastor also taught the people knowledge, weighing and studying and arranging many proverbs with great care. The Pastor sought to find words of delight, and uprightly he wrote words of truth.

> The words of the wise are like goads, and like nails firmly fixed are the collected sayings; they are given by one Shepherd. My son, beware of anything beyond these. Of making many books there is no end, and much study is a weariness of the flesh.
>
> The end of the matter; all has been heard. Fear God and keep his commandments, for this is the whole duty of man. For God will bring every deed into judgment, with every secret thing, whether good or evil. (12:9–14)

We have now come to the last three paragraphs of the book. Unfortunately, it is pretty common to claim that this passage represents a new author trying to make the work of the main body of Ecclesiastes palatable to pious sensibilities by tacking this on as an addendum, but that is simply not compatible with the fact that the Bible is a divinely inspired book.

This closing statement fits quite well with what the Bible says about Solomon. He is *qoheleth*, "the Convener," the shepherd king of the assembly. Read 1 Kings 8:12 and following to see Solomon's role in leading the people in worship at the temple he made, and you will see how appropriate it is to give him that title.

Furthermore, Solomon was known as one who could and did "find words of delight," who "uprightly . . . wrote words of truth." As the Queen of Sheba exclaimed, "Happy are your men! Happy are your servants, who continually stand before you and hear your wisdom!" (1 Kings 10:8).

> And God gave Solomon wisdom and understanding beyond measure, and breadth of mind like the sand on the seashore, so that Solomon's wisdom surpassed the wisdom of all the people of the east and all the wisdom of Egypt. For he was wiser than all other men, wiser than Ethan the Ezrahite, and Heman, Calcol, and Darda, the sons of Mahol, and his fame was in all the surrounding nations. He also spoke 3,000 proverbs, and his songs were 1,005. He spoke of trees, from the cedar that is in Lebanon to

> the hyssop that grows out of the wall. He spoke also of beasts, and of birds, and of reptiles, and of fish. And people of all nations came to hear the wisdom of Solomon, and from all the kings of the earth, who had heard of his wisdom. (1 Kings 4:29–34)

A wise man in the Bible is one who preserves, teaches, and arranges for the proper transmission of his wisdom to others; thus the importance of "words of delight" and "weighing and studying and arranging many proverbs with great care." Solomon himself has written about the importance of communicating through appropriate words: "A word fitly spoken is like apples of gold in a setting of silver" (Prov. 25:11). The idea here (12:10 especially) is that Solomon composed sayings that are elegant and pleasing in form and therefore able to convey faithful meaning. Here is something Solomon labored at. He worked at finding the right words. It didn't just come to him. It was difficult.

While these words are "words of delight," their meaning is not necessarily pleasant. As a "shepherd," Solomon's words work like "nails" that are well-placed, "like goads" that herd the congregation. Remember what a goad is—a pointed stick that a shepherd or herdsman uses to jolt the sheep or cattle to keep them from falling off a cliff or from running into some other hazard. Goads are painful but necessary. The wisdom of Solomon is not always comfortable. It confronts reality without shrinking from life's dark side.

The second phrase is parallel. The ESV, like the NIV, translates it as "collected sayings," but it is more like "the collections of Masters," meaning of the "masters/teachers of assemblies." The writings and books these wise masters record and collect are ultimately the means by which the divine herder gathers and leads his sheep. The one Shepherd is represented by many under-shepherds. "And I will give you shepherds after my own heart, who will feed you with knowledge and understanding" (Jer. 3:15).

The fact that choosing the right words takes such diligence and skill means that one should be cautious about trying to write down more wisdom (12:12). Solomon's statement about "making many books" (which might better be translated "of making collections of writings") is often understood as if Solomon would be scandalized by Borders, Barnes & Noble, or Amazon.com. There are a couple of interpretive options here.

The first option is that Solomon is asserting the sufficiency of the words of the wise. This would stress for us the importance of knowing the Bible. Solomon and the divine Shepherd have wisely given their instruction; there is no need to go beyond it. That is, it would be wrong to try to transcend it with something that deals with these issues more thoroughly or more accurately.

Whether or not this is precisely Solomon's meaning, we would do well to consider the idea. Scripture *is* sufficient. Particularly, wisdom literature is sufficient, as far as words go, for raising children in wisdom. It is here (12:10) that Solomon appeals to "my son," tying his words to other things he has written. The recipient of much of wisdom literature is the son, the one who is to learn to rule wisely from his father (Prov. 1:8, 10, 15; 2:1). We have every reason to believe that the proverbs and wisdom literature are important for the growth of our Christian children.

Contrast this idea with what has often happened in Protestant church history, where not wisdom literature but doctrinal and ethical catechisms were taught to children. Instead of wise sayings carefully arranged by God's own Spirit, doctrinal formulations and definitions were expected to be memorized. Surely, if God had thought it was so important to expose children to a correct catechism, he would have written one himself. "Beware of anything beyond these." God knows what is needed for our children to learn wisdom.

The second option for understanding Solomon's warning here (and the one I favor) is to interpret him as telling us that to arrive at this kind of wisdom demands more than you can probably give to the venture. The warning here is not against writing books nor is it to be taken, as it so often is, as a whining complaint about the number of books that are out there. If you want to add to Solomon's wisdom, then writing a book like this demands unending trouble and work.

In keeping with his claim to have searched to find just the right words (12:10), the writer is telling us that it is not easy to put together a collection of wise sayings like you have just read. Do not be fooled. It affects the body as well ("much study is weariness to the flesh"). Do not be tempted to willy-nilly add your own wisdom to this book because wisdom comes by hard experience and suffering. It does not come naturally or easily. When Solomon addresses the reader as "my son," we understand that his point is that to be a true son one must emulate the father/master—Solomon and his deep personal wrestling with life. Those who are being groomed to rule after the pattern of their father (teacher) must reckon with the difficulty of passing on wisdom through one's writing.

Finally, Solomon concludes *fear God and keep his commands, for this is man's all*. This is man's all. This is all we are to do in the face of a *hebel* existence. Man is put in his proper place in Solomon's writing. Fearing God, paradoxically, is the way to live without fear. All of our anxieties about a life we cannot predict or control are banished before God who controls all.

> I perceived that whatever God does endures forever; nothing can be added to it, nor anything taken from it. God has done it, so that people fear before him. (Eccl. 3:14)
>
> For when dreams increase and words grow many, there is [vapor]; but God is the one you must fear. (Eccl. 5:7)
>
> Though a sinner does evil a hundred times and prolongs his life, yet I know that it will be well with those who fear God, because they fear before him. (Eccl. 8:12)
>
> But it will not be well with the wicked, neither will he prolong his days like a shadow, because he does not fear before God. (Eccl. 8:13)

The reason for fear is that God will judge every deed good and bad, open and secret. While this may be a reason for fearing God, it is actually the conclusion we *wanted* to hear from Solomon's honest look at life's uncontrollable nature. Everything that is done will be judged. That means that nothing is meaningless or ultimately vanity, and it all can be understood and it all fits in God's wisdom. Time and events are not vapor for God, only for us.

This book ends with the Hebrew word *ra'* ("trouble," "disaster," "calamity," or "evil"). Ecclesiastes begins with *hebel* ("vapor") and *ra'* (1:2–13) and ends with *hebel* and *ra'* (12:8–14). These are the two characteristics of our world under the sun. We are creatures, so everything is *hebel*. We are fallen, guilty creatures, sons and daughters of Adam, so the curse of evil (*ra'*) is omnipresent and inescapable.

You will continue to hear preachers explain Ecclesiastes as the perspective of the unbeliever, the cynic, the pessimist. You will hear them offer Ecclesiastes as an evangelistic tool to help the unbeliever learn of his own meaningless life, as if Solomon reaches his depths when he writes vapor of vapors, all is vapor.

With these final words Solomon reaches the pinnacle of believing wisdom. These are truly words of faith. Solomon had learned, as we all must, that he was not in control. Thus we learn that as creatures we cannot trust time and events. We have no leverage over them. As we are time-bound, dust-bound creatures living under the sun, and as we are sons and daughters of Adam who will never escape God's comprehensive curse in this life, so we will never be completely "in the know," never satisfied, never free from the trouble and calamity, never escape death in this life.

Never.

This is just as much true for those who are believers as anyone else! Our only hope is in the living God, our Maker and our Savior. Our hope now is clearer than it was for Solomon, but our calamitous, vaporous situation under the sun is no different.

> For I consider that the sufferings of this present time are not worth comparing with the glory that is to be revealed to us. For the creation waits with eager longing for the revealing of the sons of God. For the creation was subjected to futility, not willingly, but because of him who subjected it, in hope that the creation itself will be set free from its bondage to decay and obtain the freedom of the glory of the children of God. For we know that the whole creation has been groaning together in the pains of child-

birth until now. And not only the creation, but we ourselves, who have the firstfruits of the Spirit, groan inwardly as we wait eagerly for adoption as sons, the redemption of our bodies. For in this hope we were saved. Now hope that is seen is not hope. For who hopes for what he sees? But if we hope for what we do not see, we wait for it with patience. (Rom. 8:18–25)

Suggested Readings & Resources

Johnston, Robert K. "Confessions of a Workaholic: A Reappraisal of Qoheleth." *Catholic Biblical Quarterly* 38 (1976): 17–28.

Jordan, James B., Peter J. Leithart, et al. *Ecclesiastes and Wisdom Literature*. 15th Annual Biblical Horizons Bible Conference, taped lectures. Niceville, FL: Biblical Horizons, 2005. Available from Biblical Horizons, P.O. Box 1096, Niceville, FL 32588.

Jordan, James B. *From Bread to Wine: Toward a More Biblical Liturgical Theology*. Niceville, FL: Biblical Horizons, 2001. Available from Biblical Horizons, P.O. Box 1096, Niceville, FL 32588.

_______. Primeval Saints: Studies in the Patriarchs of Genesis. Moscow, ID: Canon Press, 2001.

_______. *Through New Eyes: Developing a Biblical View of the World*. Brentwood, TN: Wolgemuth & Hyatt Publishers, Inc., 1988.

Kaiser, Walter C., Jr. *Ecclesiastes: Total Life. Everyman's Bible Commentary*. Chicago: Moody Bible Institute, 1979.

Luther, Martin, "Notes on Ecclesiastes," in *Luther's Works, Volume 15*, ed. Jaroslav Pelikan and Helmut T. Lehmann. St. Louis, MO: Concordia Publishing House and Philadelphia: Fortress Press, 1955-86.

Ogden, Graham. *Qoheleth*. Sheffield, England: JSOT Press, 1987.

Wilson, Douglas. *Joy at the End of the Tether: The Inscrutable Wisdom of Ecclesiastes*. Moscow, ID: Canon Press, 1999.

Wright, J. Stafford. "The Interpretation of Ecclesiastes" in *Classical Evangelical Essays in the Old Testament*, ed. Walter C. Kaiser, Jr. Grand Rapids, MI: Baker Book House, 1972.